HITTING YOUR
STRIDE

DATE DUE

OTHER TITLES IN THE CAPITAL
CAREER & PERSONAL DEVELOPMENT SERIES:

THE 10 LENSES: Your Guide to Living & Working in a Multicultural World by Mark A. Williams

BE HEARD THE FIRST TIME: The Woman's Guide to Powerful Speaking by Susan Miller

FIT IN! The Unofficial Guide to Corporate Culture by Mark A. Williams

MANAGER MECHANICS: People Skills for the First-Time Manager by Eric P. Bloom

MENTAL AGILITY: The Path to Persuasion by Robert L. Jolles

MILLION DOLLAR NETWORKING by Andrea Nierenberg

NONSTOP NETWORKING by Andrea Nierenberg

NOW WHAT DO I DO? The Woman's Guide to a New Career by Jan Cannon

SAVVY INTERVIEWING: How to Ace the Interview & Get the Job by John Van Devender and Gloria Van Devender-Graves

THE SAVVY PART-TIME PROFESSIONAL: How to Land, Create, or Negotiate the Part-Time Job of Your Dreams by Lynn Berger

SLEEPING WITH YOUR BUSINESS PARTNER: A Communication Toolkit for Couples in Business Together by Becky L. Stewart-Gross, PhD, & Michael J. Gross, EdD

SOLD! Direct Marketing for the Real Estate Pro by Lois K. Geller

WIN WITHOUT COMPETING! Career Success the Right Fit Way by Arlene R. Barro, PhD

Save 25% when you order any of these and other fine Capital titles from our website: www.capital-books.com.

HITTING YOUR
STRIDE

YOUR WORK, YOUR WAY

Nan S. Russell

Capital Career & Personal Development Series

CAPITAL
BOOKS, INC.
Sterling, Virginia

Capital Books, Inc.
P.O. Box 605
Herndon, Virginia 20172-0605

ISBN 13: 978-1-933102-56-6

Library of Congress Cataloging-in-Publication Data
Russell, Nan S.
  Hitting your stride : your work, your way / Nan S. Russell.—
1st ed.
      p. cm.—(Capital career & personal development series)
  Includes bibliographical references.
  ISBN 978-1-933102-56-6 (alk. paper)
  1. Career development. 2. Success in business. 3. Job satisfaction. I.
Title. II. Series.

  HF5381.R7893 2007
  650.1—dc22

                                        2007039006

Printed in the United States of America on acid-free paper that meets the American National Standards Institute Z39-48 Standard.

First Edition

10 9 8 7 6 5 4 3

This book is dedicated to Dan S. Russell,
my husband and best friend . . .
you rekindle my light,
encourage my dreams,
and make me laugh.
I love you.

"Sometimes our light goes out, but is blown into flame by another human being. Each of us owes deepest thanks to those who have rekindled this light."
Albert Schweitzer

CONTENTS

ACKNOWLEDGMENTS

*"Love life, engage it, give it all you've got. Love it with a
passion, because life truly does give back, many times over,
what you put into it."* **Maya Angelou**

A friend happened to e-mail this Maya Angelou quote
to me on the day I was struggling with how best to
write an expression of gratitude to so many who nurtured,
helped, assisted, and believed this book into existence. It
captures my feelings. I am the grateful recipient of life's
multiplying abundance in the birthing of this book.

I am indebted to my agent, Lisa Hagan, president of
Paraview Inc., who believed in this project from the beginning, persisting until she found just the right home with
Capital Books, where publisher, Kathleen Hughes, and senior editor, Amy Fries, helped me better craft, shape, and
polish it into existence. Along with my appreciation for the
sales and marketing team at Capital Books, I send special
thanks to Steve and Bill Harrison for their promotional
insights and quantum-leap coaching.

I am also obligated to the bosses, staffs, peers, and co-
workers I've worked with during my career, especially at
QVC, Comcast, and Macy's. They pushed me to grow,
trusted me to lead, challenged me to improve, and forced
me from my comfort zone. Without them, there would be
fewer anecdotes to share, lessons learned, or reflections
gained, and many of my "winning at working" philosophies
might not have evolved. Sometimes we struggled, not
seeing eye-to-eye; sometimes we soared, creating projects

and businesses together; but always we learned from each other. I am grateful that we worked together and for all I have learned from them.

A group of family and friends offered me insights and encouragement in conceiving and writing this book. Each, in a special way, contributed to its outcome—supporting and encouraging my dreams or challenging my thinking; keeping me focused or brainstorming its concepts; supporting the research or organizing my efforts; offering new insights or nurturing my body and soul. My personal thanks to Ian Russell, Janine Russell, Neva Russell, Craig Schindler, Heidi Schindler, Marlene Robinson, Dana Maranz, Diane Hennessy, Kat DeVall, Debbie Lewellen, Faye Kurren, Connie Callahan, and Marianne Kaplan. Plus, to the many readers of my columns, "Winning at Working" and "In the Scheme of Things," who wrote to tell me my words were making a difference in their lives—thank you for keeping me writing.

In after-dinner debates and discussions at the kitchen table while growing up, my father, Frank Schindler, taught me the human side of business—and along with my mother, Nancy Schindler—laid the foundational values of persistence and determination and a good-to-your-word work ethic that shaped me. Their encouragement, love, and confidence are touchstones for my life. While my father did not live to see his shy daughter hitting her stride, it was first by following his footsteps that I discovered my own, and then by his example that I sought my own life's music.

While it is an understatement, I'd like to state for the record to Beth Pelkofsky, "I couldn't have done this book without you." Beth has many gifts, but the one I especially appreciated is her honest feedback. I counted on her to tell me if a chapter wasn't good enough, if I missed the message, or if I touched her heart. I looked to her to push back when it didn't "feel" right, so I could adjust my approach to enhance understanding. From proposal ideas to chapter input, from tracking to editing, from researching to verifying, Beth was my project partner. But long before this book, she was my friend. Delivering this book together has only deepened that friendship.

I dedicated this book to my husband, Dan, not for his amazing support, technical assistance, encouragement, patience, and first-reader critiques, without which, this book would never have made its debut. And not for nudging me to persist when the sting of rejection dampened my resolve, or offering his hand when I stumbled. No, I dedicated this book to my husband of nearly thirty-three years because he nurtures my spirit and welcomes me to play the music in my soul. It was through Dan's unconditional mirror of love that I embraced my gifts and talents and found the courage to be me. Mark Twain said, "To get the full value of joy you must have someone to divide it with." Dan is my someone.

With humble appreciation to the many who made this book come to life,

Nan S. Russell
Whitefish, Montana

INTRODUCTION:
INSIGHTS TO THIS BOOK

"The highest reward for man's toils is not what he gets from it, but what he becomes by it." **John Ruskin**

Zebra and giraffe scattered as the six-seater plane taxied on a dirt tarmac in the Linyanti-Savuti channel region of Botswana's Okavango Delta. Brian, our guide, waited in an open Land Rover under an acacia's shade, eager to show us the wonders of Kings Pool safari camp and animal reserve. It was there we met the cheetah and the leopard.

Many people find it difficult to discern between the two, but Brian taught us a bush way. "Leopards are special animals," he said, pointing to a leopard and her cub, basking in what remained of the sunlight, atop an empty termite mound. "You can tell how special," he continued, "because the leopard was given a protective necklace. Take a look." Sure enough, dark markings giving the appearance of a necklace graced her neck.

"But the cheetah wasn't given such a gift," he continued. "That's why she's crying." The next day when Brian spotted a cheetah, and the Land Rover maneuvered us near enough to view her face without binoculars, the black tear marks were apparent.

Experiencing the African bush enlarged my perspective and understanding about life's harmony. So when Capital Books suggested a cover design that included a cheetah, it delighted me. Of course, I told publisher Kathleen Hughes, "Our cheetah's tears are tears of joy because she's hitting her stride."

The cheetah may not have received a necklace, but she got a different gift. When she's hitting her stride, she's flying, without feet touching the ground, at speeds unmatched. You can fly, too, when your gifts and talents are offered through your work.

My hope is that this book speeds your journey to finding and hitting your unique stride, enhances your work life, encourages you to live your life's dreams, and, in the words of thirteenth-century philosopher Rumi, helps you find your wings:

> You were born with potential
> You were born with goodness and trust.
> You were born with ideals and dreams.
> You were born with greatness.
> You were born with wings.
> You are not meant for crawling, so don't.
> You have wings.
> Learn to use them and fly.

I wrote *Hitting Your Stride* for my son, Ian, and his friends and his friends' friends, and his wife, Janine, and her sisters and their friends. I wrote it for my nieces and nephews, and the sons and daughters of my friends and relatives. I wrote it for clients, business associates, staff, and co-workers. I wrote it for you. It's an offer of insights learned by one generation passed to another.

This is not a book of answers—or ideals from an outside perspective looking in. I've been there. I know what it's like. I know how hard work can be. This is a book of lessons shared, insights gained, and ideas and suggestions gleaned while maneuvering from a minimum-wage employee to a vice president of a $4.4 billion dollar company, receiving sixteen promotions along the way, eleven self-created or created around my talents; achieving a dream of living and writing from the mountains of Montana before fifty; and actively continuing to invent the future I want to face.

It's not a how-to book about a resume-building career.

I was fired from my first professional job and passed over for a coveted department-head promotion I'd worked years to attain; I got caught up in naive wishful thinking and lost my way when I was seduced by power and trappings. I know firsthand the potholes, sinkholes, soul-suckers, and motivation-drainers of having a job that affects self-esteem, confidence, and well-being. But I also know the exuberance of *hitting your stride*, offering your gifts, and inventing your future. I share a mix of both in the hopes of helping you achieve what you want for your life.

What's in it for me? The satisfaction in making a difference in some small way, in giving back, in sharing honestly so the next generation can achieve their dreams and life's potential. Plus, if you like this book, there'll be opportunities for me to write more, and I do like book writing.

The majority of business books fall into three categories: leadership, management, and business life (where this one falls). Most are written by consultants, trainers, motivational speakers, academics, celebrity CEOs, or well-known coaches. Or, as one Amazon reviewer comments, "A book from yet another management guru who never served a day as a real manager, of a real company."

This book is different. I've spent over twenty-five years in the work trenches. I've managed over five hundred people, helped transform a company culture for ten thousand, was an advisor to hundreds of line managers as well as a company president, succeeded in both support and line management roles, and achieved a life dream in the process.

Even so, I'm not going to tell you how to be successful or what success is, because what success is for you is not the same as it is for me. When I shared my Montana dream with colleagues, I frequently heard, "Why would you want to do that?" But it's what I wanted for *my* life. Which, of course, is the key to all this. *Hitting your stride* is not about your career, it's about your life.

I'm not going to encourage or discourage company ladder climbing, big company or small company environments, or career progression. I don't know if one makes more sense than another for your life. I'm not out to convince you there are ten easy steps to discovering work happiness or financial freedom. Instead, I'm offering a smorgasbord of *winning at working* lessons I learned the hard way. Use what makes sense for you, and throw away the rest. My approach is to show you what something "looks like," so if you decide to use an idea or insight, you can. I never found it useful to be told what I should do, because what another person meant and what I thought they meant often differed. So, I'm sharing what worked and didn't work for me and hundreds like me, offering a glimpse through anecdotes, commentary, and reflective exercises. This is a read-tonight, use-tomorrow common-sense, but uncommon-practice approach. Start with a chapter that interests you and proceed in any order.

While some stories shared are personal, many are drawn from years of management experience with thousands of employees in a couple dozen states. I've even included a postscript with a bit of a boss's perspective.

Now for the disclaimer and cautionary note—you know the type, the one in which I disclaim any reference to specific people or places. Of course I make such a declaration because the majority of examples are composites of knowledge accumulated over a few decades. Since I have worked for a specific number of companies (a dozen), and the people I have worked with are finite, it's okay to assume my experience was cemented in those organizations. Still, today I speak and consult in addition to write, so I'm around a growing number of people and companies. If you're certain you recognize yourself, or someone else, or some event because you knew me along the way, or know me now, remember it's possible, but still unlikely.

Hitting Your Stride: Your Work, Your Way exemplifies a *winning at working* philosophy that's evolved from my first job as a poolside snack-bar attendant at sixteen, to starting my own company four decades later. *Winning at working* is when, with or without climbing the company hierarchy, you bring the best of who you are to work, creating your own luck, differentiating your work performance, and making a difference. Interesting work and financial rewards follow. But I didn't always understand it that way. I used to approach my work anything but my way, with usually one goal in mind. Here's a glimpse.

The sound of wood-on-wood sealed the outcome even without seeing the orange-striped ball roll past the wicket. "I don't want to play croquet with her," the division vice president laughed as she offered consolation iced tea to the players gathered for team-building. She added, "Congratulations! I had no idea you were so competitive."

She was right. I liked to win and had the ribbons, trophies, and notches on my resume to back it up. My competitive standard of personal performance equated "As" in school or the highest ratings at work with success, and anything less in this binary self-evaluation system as failure.

Years later, reacquainted in a work relationship with a colleague from my early days, I was surprised when he told me, "I didn't like you when we worked together before. You were too intense, only wanting to win." He softly added, "You're different now." He's right. I am different. Thankfully, I've evolved in twenty-something years, although my daughter-in-law, defeated in a holiday game of Monopoly, probably still labels me competitive. I like the fun of winning, but I see it differently now.

Somewhere along the line I realized I was playing the wrong game. At first, I played the want-everyone-to-like-me game. Then graduated to the need-to-be-perfect game, augmented by the accomplishments-equal-personal-value game. What I should have been playing all along was my best-life game. I realized achievements, promotions, bank accounts, and trophies are not the measures for that one.

My best-life is both simpler and harder to play, and I'm finding it's not a game at all. It's a onetime opportunity to offer me-ness, my uniqueness, to the world. Like a mentor of mine who mirrored a wall in her office so she could look herself in the eye after tough decisions, I want to look my life in the eye and know I offered the best "me" to the world. Today, that's my definition of winning. That's what I'd like to help you do as well—to offer your best "you" to the world. Why? It makes for a better world for all of us. It's when we're all winning, that we *all* win. For me, that's a vision worth working towards.

Hitting Your Stride integrates *winning at working* philosophies, behaviors, and principles into its pages. The phrase, "hitting your stride," is shorthand for what it looks like for you to be *winning at working*. When you're *winning at working* . . . when you're *hitting your stride* . . . no one needs to tell you. You know you're doing it by how it feels. It's working with ease and grace, the rhythm of your gifts coming through in their soul-filled splendor. It's your pace, your talents, your highest "you" shining through.

Like the cheetah, when you're *hitting your stride*, your feet are off the ground. You can both lose yourself in, and reveal yourself through, your work. My wish is that work struggles are short, and work joys are abundant. If that's what you want from your work, this book is for you.

PART ONE

UNCOMMON PRACTICE

"Common sense is not so common."
Voltaire

1
CREATING YOUR OWN LUCK

"Opportunities are seldom labeled." **John A. Shedd**

I thought I was ready for what the world had to offer me. But, with an undergraduate degree from Stanford and a masters from the University of Michigan, I was fired from my first professional job. What I learned next was the foundation for a successful career. I learned the hard way, discovering firsthand the power of creating my own luck.

I decided to find an interim position while I looked for a *real* one. Against friends' advice, I accepted a temporary position at minimum wage in an industry I knew little about. I decided the way to enjoy the position was to learn everything I could and contribute all I could. I poured over manuals in my downtime, developed processes to expedite the work, trained new employees, volunteered for additional assignments, and did anything that needed to be done.

Four weeks into a ten-week job, I was unexpectedly offered my first management position—a position that led to five promotions in the next seven years. It turns out I was creating my own luck, although I didn't know it then, just by doing simple things many people fail to do. This chapter shares what I learned.

WHAT IT MEANS TO CREATE YOUR OWN LUCK
When you consistently and positively differentiate your performance, you create personal luck in the workplace. But people confuse luck with chance. Chance is me getting a

hole in one. It's "something that happens unpredictably without discernible human intention or observable cause," according to *Merriam-Webster's*.

We're benefactors or victims of chance—finding a ten-dollar bill, being in a fender bender, getting in the shortest but slowest line at the grocery store. We're at the right or wrong place at the right or wrong time. Chance is out of our hands. Newspapers are filled with comic, tragic, frightening, and astonishing chance occurrences. Philosophically, it is what it is and can profoundly change lives.

Luck is different. You have everything to do with it. You create it. The quality and quantity of work you do, the impressions you leave, and the results you get influence future "lucky" moments and opportunities. Everyday, you help or hinder your interests at work, often not knowing it. *Merriam-Webster's* defines luck as "a force that brings good fortune or adversity." It's "the events or circumstances that operate for or against an individual." And here's the key: you're that force.

Are you unlucky if you get lung cancer after a lifetime of smoking? Yes, compared to millions of smokers who don't. But a smoker has a luck-factor less than someone who never smoked. Just like my husband, a committed runner, has a healthy heart luck-factor higher than couch or mouse-potatoes his age.

It's the same at work. You control your luck-factor. You increase or decrease the likelihood of opportunity, enjoyable work, and goal achievement. What I've found in twenty years of managing is most people decrease, not increase, their luck-factor. Most people settle. They do what they need to do to get by. They opt out of *creating* luck. And they fail to do simple things that differentiate their performance.

Of course, simple doesn't mean easy. It's simple to understand that if you expend more calories than you take in, you'll lose weight. But if it were easy to do that consistently, there wouldn't be an obesity epidemic. *Knowing* how to differentiate performance and create luck will get you as far at work as it does knowing how to lose weight.

Nowhere. It's not the knowing most people need, it's the *doing*. That's the first and most important component to any luck creation. Doing. The founder of McDonald's, Roy Kroc, put it this way: "Luck is a dividend of sweat. The more you sweat, the luckier you get." I know that to be true, too. What you'll find in this chapter, and throughout the book, are specific luck ingredients I personally experienced in my career or in the careers of thousands of people I observed, advised, and worked with as I moved from a minimum-wage employee to vice president of a four-billion-dollar company.

There are many ways to create luck. But in work as in clothes, one size doesn't fit all. Personalize and adapt anything you find interesting or helpful to meet your style, needs, and goals.

ONE REASON REAL PEOPLE GET AHEAD

Of course, all people are real. But if your father is chairman of the board or CEO of a Fortune 500 company, your experience and exposure are different from most. Your skills may or may not be more developed, but you have the equivalent of an all-access backstage pass with unique experiences grooming you for business interactions that are out of reach for most of us.

On the other hand, if you're like me, growing up without that backstage pass to business, this section is for you. As the daughter of a credit union manager and an elementary-school secretary in a southern California town of ninety thousand, I couldn't take my eyes off the skyscrapers on my first New York business trip and had to watch my host to navigate the silverware surrounding my lunch plate at Tavern on the Green. I entered the business world with little business savvy and experienced firsthand how *real* people, those without backstage business passes, can get ahead.

The answer? *Initiative*. It's the single most powerful way to create your own luck. That's because initiative is a rare commodity in the workplace. People with initiative stand out in a sea of just-enough-to-get-byness. Initiative is not about doing your job well. That's a given. If you're not do-ing the job you're paid to do at a good or very good level, all the initiative in the world is misdirected. Do your job. Do it well. *Then* do more.

Initiative is doing the stuff no one is expecting or tell-ing or asking you to do. It involves "work at your discre-tion." That means doing what needs doing, and doing what is helpful and beneficial without being prompted. "At your discretion work" is always *in addition* to responsibilities you already have.

Initiative is why some people love working and seldom get bored. Being bored is a clue that you're expecting in-teresting work and rewarding activities to flow to you from the outside rather than be created by you. You put the con-trol in someone else's hands. But ultimately, you're in charge of your thinking, your interest level, and your life. Initiative starts when you shift your perspective and take control.

Initiative comes in large, medium, and small incre-ments. E-mailing your boss by the end of the day the an-swer to a question he had asked at a meeting (but no one could answer) demonstrates initiative. So does deciding to solve an inefficient workflow process by getting input from teammates and developing a suggested approach that others can react to. So does volunteering for a new project, or drafting an idea with detailed plans and an ini-tial test.

Opportunity is everywhere and anywhere. Leveraging it requires personal enterprise and spotting ideas. Here are a few places to look:

- ★ **Between the Cracks.** It's not part of your depart-ment (or job), and it's not part of my department (or job), but things falling through the cracks af-fect us both as well as the company. Solution— pick up, solve, or take responsibility for some.
- ★ **Ask.** I love when staff members say, "I need more to do" or "I'm interested in what you discussed at the meeting, can I get involved?" or "Is there

anything I can do to help?" Tell your boss you'd like more responsibility or ask for more work. I had an assistant who worked very quickly. She frequently asked what else she could do, and as a result, she ended up with higher-level projects and more interesting work. All because she asked.

★ **Meetings.** Meetings are filled with wish lists, visionary ideas, and/or problems requiring solutions that may fall within your expertise. Set your listening cues to pick up what you could do, not just what you need to do.

★ **Eclectic Places.** Seeds are everywhere: conferences, newspapers, magazines, the Internet, TV, sporting events, shopping centers. Incorporating concepts from one medium or venue to another can produce interesting applications.

I collect ideas and keep idea logs. It's had big paybacks for me. Hundreds of ideas pass through our heads each day. I'm not talking about world-changing ideas, but everyday "lightbulb" or curiosity moments. Train yourself to recognize and record them. Idea singles, not just home runs, can add up to a winning strategy.

When something pops to mind, log it. It may be just a snippet of an idea, but put it down. Borrow and build from other ideas because what someone else is doing may have application to your work. My lists are filled with column topics, website enhancements, marketing ideas, future books, personal development concepts, staff projects, business ideas, fun getaways, and life to-dos. If you develop a discipline to capture, nurture, and use ideas, it will dramatically affect your results. Of course, not every idea is good enough to warrant your time and effort; not every idea can be executed without approval or a nod of "okay."

Here's an example of a positive outcome. Jen came with a proposal to fix a black hole between our department and marketing, even offering to take responsibility for the procedural solution, if needed. I met with the marketing head to discuss Jen's recommendations. We agreed her proposal was a good one, and fixing the problem benefited both departments. Jen's initiative worked.

Jen often presented proposals and thus developed a reputation for solving "between-the-cracks" problems. As a result, she was asked to head a team to eliminate company black holes. The team reduced costs, increased efficiencies, and improved workflow. In time, a new department, headed by Jen, was created.

Initiative is not an attribute only some people have. Everyone has it. Visit any craft fair, hobbyist group, volunteer organization, or Internet blog. Take note of poets, musicians, artists, athletes, hackers, spammers, and graffiti artists. Initiative manifests itself in many ways and many places, positive and negative. People work on novels after a full day's work. That's initiative. They develop products in their garages, then determine how to manufacture and market them. That's initiative. Coaching your daughter's soccer team is initiative, too. So is almost everything you do involving your interests or passion.

It's curious how people can be so enterprising outside of work, yet leave it at the workplace door. Why be any less at work than who you are on weekends or evenings? Life is not just what happens outside of work. Applying that same action-oriented energy to the workplace will dramatically improve your results.

But here's the thing: initiative needs context. You build context by building experience. I learned in first grade that one plus one equals two. But, that's not the right equation when counting work experience. We often think we're building experience to help us get ahead. In reality, we're passing time. Ten years working, like a cloned Bill Murray in *Groundhog Day*, is not ten-years' worth of experience. Doing the same thing again and again yields an experience formula more like: ten times one equals one.

I used to equate years of work with years of experience. No more. I learned by making plenty of hiring and promotion mistakes, the two are not equal. Neither are years of work and performance. Doing something for five, ten, or twenty years doesn't make you automatically five, ten, or twenty years better than when you started. I've been cooking for thirty years, but I remain a mediocre cook.

Two or three years involved with a business start-up or a new project might provide more growth and knowledge than ten years in a stable venue. And it might not. Gaining experience is more about you and your approach than anything else.

Recurring work events can be predictable, boring, and unchallenging ways of passing years at work, if what you're doing is updating last year's memo, tweaking last year's budget, or fine-tuning last year's goals without applying innovation, analysis, or critical thinking. Retiring on the job is as prolific as spam and will get you as blocked as those unwanted e-mails.

I've found the difference between people who are *winning at working* and people who aren't is the difference between passing another year at work versus gaining another year of work experience. Those who build their experiences build their futures. And you can build experience without ever changing jobs.

Building experience involves the depth, diversity, challenges, and learning you gain by offering the best of who you are at work. It's seizing and creating opportunities. It's continual self-improvement and constant self-feedback.

You know you're gaining true experience when you problem solve your own mistakes, use hard-earned knowledge to handle more complex issues, make contributions more valuable than the year before, acquire new skills by venturing outside a comfort zone, embrace new ideas or technologies, or recognize you don't know as much as you thought.

People with initiative try new things, push the envelope, pitch ideas, offer innovative problem solving, and never stop learning and growing. They're the people gaining experience and building their work future.

THE POWER BEHIND IDEAS

You can have terrific initiative with outstanding ideas and never leverage it into *winning at working* results. That's because the power behind ideas lies in performance. Yours. The level of confidence people have in your ability to deliver an idea is directly related to your getting the okay to pursue it.

When you establish performance trust, you'll create for yourself opportunities on a regular basis. One successful idea delivery leads to another and another and another. Bigger and bigger ideas are entrusted to people who consistently turn ideas into reality.

Not only does an idea need to be good, but the idea-maker also needs to be a performer who can deliver the vision. That doesn't mean you need to have executed lots of ideas before getting one approved. It does mean the base quality of your work is a deciding factor. I've vetoed more good ideas than I've approved. Most were vetoed for one reason: performance trust. I didn't trust the person to deliver the idea they had. A mediocre idea from a strong performer will win approval over a great idea from someone with inconsistent follow-through and poor results.

If you can't do the little things, why would anyone give you bigger things to do? And while every idea might not be big, it takes energy, time, and resources away from other work endeavors. Not all ideas that get approved turn out to be successful. That's okay. Much is learned from the failures, too. Look at Edison and the lightbulb. But if an idea fails because it was poorly executed, we only learn the competency quotient of the initiator.

There is a mercenary side to idea approval. What happens with your idea is a reflection on the person who approved it. I know for one, I'm not willing to risk my reputation on someone's half-baked or half-executed idea. That doesn't mean I don't take risks on individuals or ideas. I do on both. Though past performance is a good indicator of future performance (most of the time), business decisions are still about odds and risks. Make sure both are in your favor. Being a strong performer is the best way to get your ideas noticed and sell them to the powers that be.

There are plenty of ideas that don't need approval. These are the ideas I start with when creating my own luck.

COMMON SENSE, UNCOMMON PRACTICE

Performance differentiation and luck creation starts with brand building. Everything you do builds your personal brand, your signature of sorts, which tells others what to expect from you. It's like any brand. If what they expect from you is not what they're looking for, you won't be the brand of choice for the assignment, the project, or the promotion.

Think of a brand you own or like, one you're passionate about. Maybe it's Starbucks Coffee or Apple's iPod or Target shopping. When you think of that brand, what attributes come to mind? Those qualities represent the brand. The same is true about brands you dislike. People create brands, too. When you hear Joe's name, you have an impression of the Joe-brand, good or not so good.

My first online class intrigued me when I noticed students' comments were more thoughtful, insightful, and connected to the material than those in a classroom. Why was that, I wondered? After my second, third, and fourth experiences with online learning, I concluded the difference was because one's name was permanently attached to the discussion log like a brand identifier. I found myself looking for certain people's names and reading their comments first because I knew their "brand" was reliable, with good information.

Remember first grade when you proudly printed your name so everyone could see it at the top of the wide-ruled paper? We may not write our names in big, bold crayon on our work anymore, but make no mistake, your brand name is on everything you do.

Building your positive brand is easier than you think. It's not only about doing things well. Sure, that's part of it. But you must also do the right things well. This section underscores eight uncommon practices learned during my career that significantly differentiate performance and create personal work-luck and positive brand building. Scores of common sense behaviors make for great uncommon work practices. Doing any will strengthen your performance. Here are eight of my favorites:

★ And Then Some
★ Taking Your Words Seriously
★ Take It or Leave It . . . But Get It
★ Those Little Things
★ A Dose of the Ds
★ Ego-Detached
★ Your ROI
★ A Bit of Pollyanna

Like most things, performance differentiation is not in the knowing, but the doing. So, if you do three or more of these behaviors consistently, you'll set yourself apart. If you do five or more consistently, you'll see a noticeable difference in performance and results. And if you do all of them, you'll significantly enhance your positive brand attributes and your ability to create your own luck.

1. And Then Some

For most of my career, a plaque hung on the wall of my cube, then of my office. It was a reminder to offer the best I had to give. Like a good-luck ritual, I read that plaque everyday. On it was the inspirational saying, "And Then Some," by Carl Holmes. It's message was powerful to this impressionable woman seeking her way in an unfamiliar business world, at a time when even a child's picture did not adorn her desk, a signal she might not be serious about her career.

Over the years, I found truth in this message. People who do their job very well "and then some" have opportunities arise that others never do. After I was fired from my first professional job, it was my doing the job, and then some, that opened a door and many like it throughout my career. Good is not good enough. You need to offer your best.

People offering to do extra work only if they get paid for it, or take on extra responsibility only if their salary is increased first, have it backwards in my book. My experience: do the work, do it well, and then do it even better.

> ### AND THEN SOME
>
> *These three little words are the secret to
> success. They are the difference between
> average people and top people in most
> companies. The top people always do what is
> expected and then some. . . . They are
> thoughtful of others; they are considerate and
> kind . . . and then some. . . . They meet their
> obligations and responsibilities fairly and
> squarely . . . and then some. . . . They are
> good friends and helpful neighbors . . . and
> then some. They can be counted on in an
> emergency . . . and then some. . . . I am
> thankful for people like this, for they make
> the world more livable, their spirit of service
> is summed up in these little words . . .
> and then some.*
> **Carl Holmes**

Higher pay, greater responsibilities, and increased opportunities follow individuals who are contributors. Anytime I look to hire people, offer permanent positions to temporary employees or interns, start up new departments or businesses, or promote individuals, I look for people doing their job well . . . and then some.

2. Taking Your Words Seriously

When we ordered a stained-glass window as an accent piece for our home, the artist-proprietor told us he was a bit behind. "So," he said, "to be on the safe side, plan on six months." That was two years ago. Each time we call or stop in, he has yet another plausible reason why our project isn't done, the appropriate apology, and a new promise of a delivery date. What he doesn't have is credibility.

Wishful promises don't cut it in small-town businesses or big-city corporations. It doesn't matter what role you're in. If you tell me you'll do something, I expect you will whether you're a business, an employee, a co-worker, or my boss. You're the one setting my expectations, so why wouldn't I believe what you tell me?

It baffles me. Few people meet or exceed the expectations they set and they control. I'm not talking about deadlines other people set for you. I'm talking about the ones you establish. Maybe it's because few people take their own words seriously. If you do, you can differentiate yourself at work. People who consistently do what they say they're going to do, without sandbagging, are memorable. They're the people with credibility. They're the ones you want to hire and promote and do business with.

People fail to establish credibility without even knowing it. If someone tells me she'll provide information by Friday, but what she meant was "around Friday," she'll feel she met her obligation to me when she pushes "send" on her e-mail Monday morning. I'll view her as lacking credibility when the information for a project I wanted was late. However, if she told me I'd get the information no later than Tuesday and delivered it on Monday, while her delivery date remains the same, her credibility soars. By managing the words that define what others can expect from you, you can surprise and delight your co-workers, bosses, and customers.

To do that, replace casual speak and wishful promises of what you'd like to have happen or believe can happen, with commitments of what will happen. But here's the key: you can't commit what you can't control. If I tell a staff member he'll get his review next week, but I only control when I finish writing it not when it's approved, the likelihood of me failing to meet an expectation I set with him is strong. But if the review is written, signed by my boss, and in for processing at the time I set the expectation, I'll meet it.

If our delinquent artisan had called three months into the project, told us he had accepted an unusual opportunity to restore an historic building and was putting other projects on hold until that was completed, and then offered us the choice of waiting until he resumed work or getting our deposit back, he could have preserved his credibility and the relationship.

Actions may speak louder than words. But it's our words that provide the backdrop for whether our actions measure up. If I'm your customer, your boss, or your co-worker, I'm taking your words seriously. I think you should, too.

3. Take It or Leave It . . . But Get It

The expense was substantial. An immersion workshop with twelve participants sharing a common goal to hone their skills. With nervous eagerness, like kindergarteners embracing school, we received feedback and suggestions about our work. Some of the comments I used. Some I didn't. But all of it was helpful.

I haven't always viewed feedback that way. At times, I've taken it more like a personal indictment than a helpful gauge; an intruder I needed to defend against, rather than input I needed to evaluate. I've even found myself akin to a workshop colleague who said he wanted input, but when he got responses different from what he expected, he argued and debated and explained. What he wanted was praise or input he agreed with, not honest reactions. It's not enough to ask for feedback. You have to be open to receive it. Our colleague's defensiveness created a willingness for us to offer nothing but cursory input. His argumentative actions lost him an opportunity for fresh voices and input.

I learned a painful lesson about feedback in my first management position. Given a large assignment, I was proud of what I had produced and certain it would be received as an outstanding product. Instead, I discovered my work was mediocre at best and significantly flawed, because I had failed to seek feedback and assessment from the end users along the way. Relying only on my thoughts and perceptions was a big mistake.

During my corporate work years, I learned to view feedback as data. The more data I got, the more information I had to improve what I was working on. Realizing I was in charge of how I used that feedback data, I learned to seek it. Feedback is opinion, not fact. It's something to evaluate, not blindly accept.

However, I find when several people have the same perception, it's good to listen. When I get insights I hadn't thought about, it's good to consider them. When input is mixed, it's good to follow my instincts. But when people provide feedback with a hatchet, finding fault rather than offering ideas for improvement, it's good to look at it with detached curiosity.

Bottom-line: if you want to differentiate your performance, learn to seek and offer well-intentioned feedback. I think of it like the Sicilian proverb: "Only your real friends will tell you your face is dirty." Let input, suggestions, and feedback be real friends to you.

4. Those Little Things

Moving to another state meant finding a new dentist. I tried one a neighbor recommended who seemed friendly and eager to please. But I never went back. His office was a case study in the importance of little things.

The coat hook was missing a screw and falling from the wall; waiting-room magazines were outdated; the posted office hours were taped over with an index card and new hours written in marker; the credenza was overflowing with mail and claim forms. There are plenty of dentists to choose from, and while he might be competent, why chance it?

It's the same at work. Bosses choose which people get the great assignments and promotions. Customers choose which businesses to frequent. All those little things really aren't so little. They're impressions. And impressions help others make decisions about you.

Does it matter if you don't spell check your e-mail? It's only an e-mail, right? Wrong. It's an impression about the way you work. Does it matter if the address label is crooked on the letter you send a customer? Who looks at the envelope, anyway? It matters. It's an impression highlighting that the company, or individual, has poor attention to detail.

Does it matter if you're habitually late for meetings or don't show up at all? I'd say so. It's an impression about what you think of other people's time. What if your voice-mail message says, "Your call is important to me. I'll get back to you as soon as I can," but then you return the phone call two weeks later. That "little thing" is an impression about the real importance of my call and your credibility.

If I ask you for a business card and you can't find one among your overflowing scraps of paper, it's a little thing. But it leaves an impression that you're disorganized. If your presentation looks like a sixth-grade term paper, it's hard to have confidence that the executed idea won't be flawed as well. How a proposal looks is a little thing that entices us to take a closer look, or not.

But, don't confuse little things with big things. You can't just do all the little things well and think that's it. Content is king on the Internet and television; competence is king in the workplace. The competent performance of your job is central to any *winning at working* philosophy. This is not a message encouraging perfectionism. You can't be perfect. If you try to be, you'll potentially limit yourself and get lost in those little things. And while some have a talent for details and noticing little things, everyone can learn.

Start by noticing those little things that create an impression on you. Little things like the cashier doesn't take off the sensor tag; or the babysitter is late again; or your name is misspelled on an invitation; or the orthodontist staff presents a rose to your daughter after her braces come off; or the repair man arrives at the designated time. What do those little things communicate to you about the person or business who delivered them? And what impressions are you leaving with your little things?

Bottom-line: If you're not paying attention to the little things, you're losing opportunities. If you want to be *winning at working*, you have to pay attention to little things, *too*.

5. A Dose of the Ds

Author and management guru Peter Drucker said, "People adjust to the level of demands made on them." I would add—we also adjust to the level we demand of ourselves. At some point, we grow up and pass for adults by how we look. To match that look with actions requires a dose of the Ds: determination and discipline.

I'll give you an example from my life. My son, Ian, was born when I was twenty-six. I decided to stay home the first two years, but needed brain stimulation and interaction with an adult world, so I decided to pursue my interest in writing. I wrote my first article, sent it to a magazine, and waited. Everyday I anxiously checked the mail to discover if today would launch my writing career. When the manuscript was finally returned with a regrets' note, my aspirations of being a writer ended. I figured an editor knew better than I did what I could do. I'd been waiting for my lightning bolt to strike.

Twenty something years later, I know success has little to do with lightning bolts. So, when I left the corporate world to live and work from the mountains of Montana, I took with me that same dream of being a writer. For six months I studied writers and writing, read books, attended seminars, and learned the business of writing.

I wanted to be a columnist, so I developed a strategy to become one by volunteering to write a life-reflections column for a regional magazine. When they agreed, my writing career was launched while I learned the discipline of column writing and fine-tuned my new craft. That column, "In the Scheme of Things" (www.intheschemeofthings .com), is now self-syndicated in several states and Canada. A second column started a year later, "Winning at Working" (www.winningatworking.com), reaches millions of web-based readers and provided the foundation for this book.

So what's the difference in today's writing success? Luck? Yes, but it's self-created luck. Better writing? Sure, I'm better today than I was in my twenties. But that's not it. It's discipline and determination. There are days when I'm not in the mood to write, but writers write, and I write. There are days when marketing my column to another publication or getting one more rejection seems overwhelming. Those days I take a deep breath before giving myself a mental kick and moving on.

People who create their own luck have discipline and determination. They push themselves to do the project when they're not in the mood, make the phone call, brush off the rejection, or learn the skill they're missing. They know there are few career lightning bolts in the world they live in.

Want to create more luck? Demand more of yourself. Stop thinking of bosses as parental, deadlines as moveable, and others as responsible for developing or motivating you. Tag, you're it!

6. Ego-Detached

With the opening of a new attraction and numerous reporters arriving in an hour, it felt like one of those "chicken-with-your-head-off" days. We were close, but not ready. So like locusts to a wheat field, a swarm of people were devouring last minute details. Then, it rained. With rain, came worms, hundreds washing onto the entrance sidewalk. When I returned to the area, I found a manager, several department supervisors, and a director outside with brooms, sweeping up worms. No one asked them to sweep worms. But with guests arriving shortly and no one else available, they found brooms and started sweeping.

They didn't get hung up over titles or roles. Instead, they did what needed to be done at the time. Their actions were what I call, ego-detached. Being ego-detached frees you to do what needs to be done because it's not about you; it's about something bigger than you. It's an attitude of contribution. How can I best serve today? How can I help? What can I contribute? Being ego-detached is taking your ego out of the picture. It's looking at the best result, not necessarily the result that's best for you.

But here's the twist. Being ego-detached is not being ego-less. I heard Donald Trump talking about egos with Larry King on CNN. He commented that all the successful people he knew had big egos, defining ego as confidence or self-esteem. Certainly believing in yourself and having high self-esteem are qualities that help to cultivate personal success. I'm not suggesting you shed either; quite the opposite. You need plenty of confidence and self-esteem in order to be ego-detached.

I learned that as a senior manager involved in a start-up company. One afternoon, the president saw me stapling information sheets in a conference room. After saying good-bye to his guest, he came back and asked, "Nan, what *are* you doing?" After explaining why meeting a FedEx pickup was critical to a corporate initiative and the number of people working to meet it, he offered to help. People who are ego-detached recognize that the best use of their time and talent can vary in the moment.

I used to marvel at colleagues of mine, other vice presidents, who delayed getting important papers to their boss because their executive assistant was gone for the day, and the papers needed to be copied. I'm not talking about the stuff that can and should wait. It's those late-night meetings when the boss says he has to review something, and he needs a copy. Ego-detached people go to the copier, copy it, and walk the copy back to their boss, regardless of title. It's how best they can serve at the moment.

Don't let your ego dictate your actions, let the situation. Don't be afraid to sweep up worms from time to time. And don't be afraid to serve. As Tolstoy put it, "The vocation of every man and woman is to serve other people." That's ego-detached.

7. Your ROI

All requests are not equal; all customers or clients are not equal; all to-do-list tasks are not equal; all work responsibilities are not equal. You can do fifty things today and get little, if any, return on your investment for having done them. Or you can do one or two things that have a large return.

You possess personal capital. It's comprised of your time, effort, knowledge, and skills. Investing that capital wisely yields a return on your investment. The higher your return on investment, your ROI, the more profit you earn. Profit in this context yields discretionary endeavors. Discretionary endeavors tap into the single most powerful thing you can do to create luck—initiative.

There are hundreds of books filled with an equal number of approaches to managing your tasks and time. Use whatever works for you. But as you do, keep your ROI in mind. Every day you invest your capital. Sometimes you invest it wisely, sometimes foolishly, sometimes neutrally. The better investments you make over time, the better your returns will be over time. Think long-term ROI. Your ROI is not about short-term gains, but sustainable long-term ones that build your brand.

Here are a few of my favorite personal ROI strategies:

* **Prioritize people over tasks.** Family or staff or a boss asking for something, regardless of what, should go to the top. Requests from your key people list should be met immediately, if possible, with a sense of urgency. These are the people who pay you the biggest dividends—love, support, and economic well-being—so do the requests from this group first, and you will build equity for the long term. When you hit life's potholes, this equity will help get you through.

* **Work smart *and* fast.** If you're slow on the computer, increase your skills. If you pace yourself or spread your work out through the day, don't. If you don't have time to train someone to help you, make the time. The more you can leverage yourself, and the more work you produce, the more valuable an asset you become and the more interesting work you'll get to do. Invest in yourself.

* **Choose making progress over being busy.** Spend a day answering e-mails, reading mail, completing miscellaneous and unimportant tasks, and at the end of the day, you'll find you're no further along on your important work than when you started. Sure, those recurring tasks need to be done, too. But choose first to make progress, then do recurring tasks, not the other way around, or

you'll find there's no time left for the big stuff that offers a better return on your investment.

★ **Go slow to go fast.** If you take the time upfront to thoughtfully set up the systems, procedures, and approaches you need to function effectively, you'll be well rewarded in the long term for your investment. This might include training, research, mission statements, or project plans. Any number of work elements fit into this category, giving you exceptional long-term returns for your upfront efforts.

If you invest your personal capital wisely, you'll find your return on investment compounding year after year and your personal stock rising.

8. A Bit of Pollyanna

"Stop being such a Pollyanna," a trusted, more experienced colleague counseled as we took the long route back to my office. He had just witnessed my project idea annihilated as co-workers eagerly argued why it wouldn't work, where it was flawed, and why it shouldn't be funded. Despite naysayers in the room that day, I believed it was worth pursuing. Ultimately, it did receive funding and became, in time, a successful endeavor. A bit of Pollyannaism got me through.

Everyday, in meetings just like this one, ideas are gutted before they're allowed to evolve. It's becoming a workplace ritual to poke pinholes in the balloon of an idea until enough air leaks out to drop it to the ground. We look first for the reasons why something can't be done; why it won't work; why it's too difficult; why it's a bad idea. We've become so good at burning idea bridges that might lead to new business, new procedures, or new products that we don't even have to build the bridges first.

People who are *winning at working* take a different approach. They pump air into idea-balloons by offering suggestions, brainstorming possibilities, and encouraging input. They point out problems by offering solutions that make the idea more viable. They're curious and intrigued, looking at how one idea might fit with another, or weaving two small ideas into one bigger one. Instead of asking why we should do this, they're encouraging people to give it a try.

Understanding the fragile nature of emerging ideas, they help protect, nurture, and greenhouse ideas—their own and others—until they have a chance to take root. They get excited about new possibilities. Often it's their optimism, vision, and positive approach that waters the seed until it grows and blooms. They have a bit of Pollyanna in them. But they probably won't call it that since Pollyanna gets a bad rap in business circles as naive and unrealistic.

I think it's time to look at Pollyanna differently. You will find more work success seeing the positive side and stretching your horizons than finding reasons not to. Impossible is often more a state of mind than a reality. As Helen Keller reminds us, "No pessimist ever discovered the secrets of the stars . . . or sailed to an uncharted land . . . or opened a new heaven to the human spirit."

But I've also learned in twenty years in management that there's more to *winning at working* than positive thinking and optimistic approaches. A bit of Pollyanna should be mixed with strong doses of common sense. Or, as British political leader Harold Wilson put it, "I am an optimist, but I'm an optimist who carries a raincoat."

Still, I know if I had listened to everyone who deflated my idea-balloons, I wouldn't have the life opportunities I have now. I've experienced the power of hope, vision, and positive thinking in the workplace. My point of view? A bit of Pollyanna is a good thing.

WHAT CAN I DO TOMORROW?

Creating luck is a process. It's developing opportunities, recognizing and embracing opportunities, and being ready when opportunities come your way. Like Oprah Winfrey says, "Luck is a matter of preparation meeting opportunity." Start preparing for yours now.

You don't need to wait until Monday or for the stars to align. You don't need to wait to get a new job or a new boss or lose twenty pounds or get organized. You can start wherever you are. Like most things, creating your own luck happens a step at a time. Below is a list of ideas to get you started. There's no prescribed order or guidelines for completion. There's no magic beyond what you put into it.

Ideas to Help You Start Creating Your Own Luck

Ideas About You:

- ★ Decide you want to.
- ★ Decide you can.
- ★ Decide you will.
- ★ Read Chapter Six: "It's All About You."
- ★ Where are you headed? How will you know if you get there? Define what *winning at working* means to you at this point in your life. Write it down. My definition has evolved dramatically over the years.
- ★ On a scale of 1-10 (1 = not at all), how bored are you at work? If your score is 4 or more, write down five reasons why and reread, "One Reason Real People Get Ahead" in this chapter. If it's less than 4, list five things that keep you interested in your job. Is there anything you can leverage from that information?

Ideas About Your Performance:

- ★ Reread your last appraisal with new eyes—ask your boss or human resources for a copy. Make a list of areas noted for improvement. Write down specifically what you're doing to address these. How are you doing? What else can you do?
- ★ If you have a job description, analyze it. Usually the most important tasks are first. Determine how your performance stacks up on the critical responsibilities. Adjust accordingly. If you don't have

a job description, write down the ten most important tasks noted on your appraisal and go from there.

★ Make progress on at least one important item on your to-do list. If you don't have a to-do list, start one.

★ Write five simple work goals for the week from a list of things you've been putting off. Do one a day. Review progress on Friday, and rewrite five for next week. And again—if they're the same goals, take smaller bites. These should be simple, doable activities like scheduling the meeting you've been putting off, calling the person you don't want to call, or reviewing the draft.

★ Read your company's annual report and marketing literature, plus information related to your department or division. Write down three ways in the position you're in, you can contribute to your organization's vision and goals.

★ Review your company's training and development curriculum, and sign up for skill development to help you do your job faster and/or smarter. If your company doesn't have a program, stop by the community college for a brochure, review online options, or check classes offered at large computer retailers.

Ideas About Your Brand Building:

★ Write down your brand attributes. Read your last performance appraisal and determine which of your attributes are apparent at work. How are these the same or different from your list? What needs to be changed or enhanced?

★ Change your voice-mail message to match your delivery and availability. Don't commit what you can't do. If you're away, adjust your message.

★ Answer all e-mails and messages from priority people (family, staff, boss).

★ Answer all e-mails and voice mails on the same day you receive them. Assess how that worked or didn't. Then, develop an ongoing strategy you can commit to. It's fine to answer an e-mail by saying that you need to research something and that you'll get back to the sender no later than X—then make sure you do.

★ Spell check every e-mail before you press send.

★ Pick three behaviors from the common sense, uncommon practices list. Reread the section and do at least a first step from each.

★ Start three idea logs—one for work, one for personal growth and development, and one for fun things to do. Log current ideas. Add at least one idea or snippet each week.

★ In addition to what you need to do, listen at meetings for what you could do. Note those ideas in your idea log as soon as you return from the meeting.

★ At a meeting or on a phone call ask, "How can I help?" Then do it.

2
Don't Be Blowing in the Wind

"If 50 million people say a foolish thing, it is still a foolish thing." **Anatole France**

I hesitated at her offer. The last two people had been fired. Her tough style and high senior-staff turnover was a company legend. Could I survive working for someone like this? Could I thrive under her leadership? Knowing others failed made me resolved not to. Knowing she was tenacious made me determined. And knowing the position was out of my comfort zone frightened me. But it *was* a great promotion. I decided if I could learn to work for her, I could work for anyone. So, I accepted.

She wasn't what I expected. Tough? Yes. Unyielding standards? Certainly. Confident? Absolutely. I watched her challenge the company president, stand her ground with the CEO, and ask a regional senior vice president to clean up his language or leave a meeting. I watched her lead with conviction and passion. She knew what she stood for and accepted no less from those working for her.

She pushed me. She challenged me. She intimidated me at times. But most of all, she amazed and inspired the best in me. In two years, her tutelage led to a regional promotion and my reluctant good-bye. I learned more about myself working for Helen than any boss before or since. I learned the importance of finding and using my own voice. And I'm indebted to her as a role model and mentor.

Working together late one night, she paused our discussion to ask, "What do you think of my mirrored wall?"

Not sure where she was going, I remarked, "Well, it makes your office seem bigger."

"Remember this Nan," she said looking more intensely at me, "some decisions you will make in your career will be tough ones—some lonely, some painful. Some will impact people and their families. Here's the best advice I can give you: answer to yourself; listen to yourself; think for yourself. Because at the end of the day, you should be able to look yourself in the eye and know you did what *you* believed was right. If you can do that, you've succeeded. That's the reason for the mirrors. Every night before I leave, I look myself in the eye." I've reflected countless times on her words.

Today, I recognize Helen's legacy stamped on my voice. From her, I learned the importance of offering my point of view, taking risks to be heard, knowing what I stand for, and speaking from my heart. Doing these made a difference in my career, and I contend it will make a difference in yours.

But it's an arduous path where I sometimes still stumble. There are days I'm the last person I want to look in the eye, not proud of my waning courage, weak voice, or conforming follower-ship. But now the difference is when I slip off the path, I know it. I feel a self-betrayal and hear the words of the German scholar Martin Luther reminding me, "You are not only responsible for what you say, but also for what you do not say."

Branded a maverick at one point in my career, I grimaced at the label. It was a time when my idealism trumped my fear. There were times my heart pounded so loudly from the fear of speaking out—I thought surely others would hear it. There were times I voiced concerns others were afraid to articulate, and times I challenged the status quo. While my ideas or suggestions or remarks were not always embraced, new opportunities emerged, and I learned an important lesson. I felt better. I could look myself in the eye at night knowing I made the right decision to speak from a well-intentioned heart.

That's key. The voice I'm talking about finding is the one

that comes from a helpful heart, an attitude of service, of support, of beneficial input. I didn't speak out for personal gain, but from a vision of making things better. That's what Helen taught me. Speak the truth as you know it, without personal-gain intent, and you won't go wrong.

Sure there are risks. Not everyone wants to hear words that challenge the status quo or make them feel uncomfortable. You may be wrong or have a limited perspective on the issues. But if you are offering the best of who you are to the workplace, eventually you can't do anything else but speak the truth.

If you want to make your work "work" for you, find and establish your own voice, develop an understanding of what issues you'll go to the mat for and which you won't, and learn how to think for yourself. Without such grounding, issues can take on lives of their own, blowing people to and fro, like tumbleweeds in the desert.

Opportunities to champion an issue can lead to interesting and meaningful work. Passion and conviction can lead to new ventures. Provocative thinking can lead to new positions.

Bottom-line: if you want to be *hitting your stride*, don't be blowing in the wind.

WHOM TO LISTEN TO

On the eve of selecting a successor to Pope John Paul II, there was a *New York Times* article headlined, "Even Cardinals Are Prone to Peer Pressure." Ah yes, I thought, aren't we all. I well remember my teenage son's proclivity for baggie pants, black boots, and nearly offensive T-shirts, and my own coveting of a foreign car suitable to blend into the executive parking lot as a newbie vice president.

In fact, according to Dr. Richard Moreland, University of Pittsburgh psychology professor, "Conformity is a big thing." There are two types: "Informational conformity, where one person believes others know best, and normative conformity, where fear of rejection or loss of status is the driving force."

Both affect results. Conformity is a bottom-line problem

for any business with more than one employee. In an era where intellectual property fuels innovation, we need the best ideas we can get. But best ideas don't happen from cloned thinking.

Results of human intellect will continue to bring profits to the bottom-line and technological and scientific breakthroughs to the world, as well as personal satisfaction and meaningful work to those involved. While thinking like everyone else at work may feel safer, group-thinkers are less valuable to companies when critical or creative thinking is required. Here's why.

As individuals, we get stuck in what we can see, imagine, and do. Groups can get stuck, too, often believing those running the departments or the businesses or the meetings, or those verbally contributing the most in them, know best. But neither rank nor verbal skill correlates with creativity, knowledge, experience, insight, or intelligence.

Group thinking is affected by both group dynamics and composition. If a meeting or department is composed mostly of analytically oriented individuals, the tendency is to see ideas or solutions in that way and shut out more creative offerings by other members, just like a room of right brainers can fail to connect with a left brainer's contribution.

Outspoken or influential individuals, unable to balance personal interests or "see" outside themselves or their groups, can sway the group from big-picture thinking. Hence, lower-level thinking can result from group work. Of course, better decisions and greater wisdom-thinking can also result with the right individuals in the right groups willing to contribute their individual thoughts. In *The Wisdom of Crowds*, James Surowiecki points out, "The real paradox of group intelligence is that groups are smartest when everyone is acting as much like an individual as possible."

That's the challenge. Your voice is needed in the workplace. It's unique. No one knows what you know in exactly the way you know it. I'm always struck when someone reframes a problem, sees a new solution, or comes up with an unusual perspective after everyone else has repeatedly looked at the same issue. I'm always struck when I hear a courageous, passionate, and grounded voice in the workplace. And I'm always struck with the powerful results that emerge when independent thinkers blend thoughts.

We are obliged by the nature of the work hierarchy to listen to certain people. Usually they include our boss and the subsequent chain of command, clients or customers, both internal and external, and our staff or team. But don't stop there. Listen to and learn from everyone you can.

But remember this—listening is not thinking, regurgitating others' thoughts is not thinking, repackaging others' opinions is not thinking. Don't confuse thinking with other mental gymnastics. Thinking is using your judgment, reasoning, and inference to attain clear ideas and reach conclusions. Thinking is work. Like most things we work at, the more we do it, the better we become, and our use-it-or-lose-it brain muscle needs to be exercised. Here are four ways.

Workout Tips for Honing Your Thinking Muscle

1. Make an Appointment with Yourself
Schedule time to think, reflect, contemplate, and dream big. I believe we have an obligation to bring our best thoughts and wisdom to this world we share. Every week I schedule a minimum three-hour block of think-time on my calendar. Friday after lunch is my time. Throughout the week, I jot down questions, and on Friday I pick one or two for in-depth thinking.

Bill Gates is known to take personal think retreats. As Henry Ford quipped, "Thinking is the hardest work there is, which is probably why so few engage in it."

2. Read. Read. Read. Read. Read.
Nonfiction. Fiction. Newspapers. Magazines. Newsletters. E-zines. Blogs. Websites. Cereal boxes. Anything. But when you do, include authors with different points of view—authors with whom you don't fully agree, who think differently from you, or who have divergent life experiences.

Reading lets you try on other people's thinking and challenge your own. It allows you to consider differing beliefs and perspectives. It helps you visualize diverse worlds and contemplate alternatives. It builds your logic, reasoning, and knowledge. It introduces you to new people and places. And it stretches your idea boundaries, enlarges your vision, and builds your ability to think clearly and creatively.

3. Cultivate a Beginner's Mind

There is a Japanese concept called "Shoshin," or "beginner's mind." Buddhist scholar Shunryu Suzuki defines it this way: "This does not mean a closed mind, but actually an empty mind and a ready mind. If your mind is empty, it is always ready for anything; it is open to everything. In the beginner's mind there are many possibilities; in the expert's mind there are few."

When you cultivate a beginner's mind, you don't come with pre-tagged baggage and a designer "I know" or "I believe" label. Instead you approach with curiosity, wonder, humility, and interest. You're willing to grow and learn from whatever comes your way as if it were the first time.

Even if you're experienced, don't close yourself to people's ideas or suggestions, or approach thinking as if you know the answer. Laurence G. Boldt, in *Zen Soup*, writes: "As only an empty cup can be filled, so only a heart emptied of the pride of what it thinks it knows can be open to new experience and receive the gifts of wisdom."

4. Crystallize and Distill

Have you ever been certain you understood your point of view until you try to explain it? Or tried to write about a topic only to find you have foggy thinking? When that happens, crystallize and distill your thoughts into one or two succinct sentences. At one time, this technique was referred to as an "elevator speech." The idea being that if you rode the elevator with the CEO for forty seconds and he asked, "What's new?" you'd be ready with a coherent and succinct answer.

My technically gifted husband uses a flow chart to help

distill his thoughts; a verbal friend records messages to herself with sound-bite phrases; and as a writer, I hone my thinking through writing. It's a way to capture my thoughts and find my voice. Use whatever works for you. Then put your "notes" aside and review them later. When you return to the list, assume the thoughts are someone else's and approach them with a beginner's mind.

It took me years to find and hear my voice, learn whom to listen to, reliably gather information, assess conflicting views, and think for myself. Until I did, I was more often than I care to admit, like a leaf off a New England fall tree, blowing in the wind, easily swept away by an intriguing speaker, a challenging boss, a passionate co-worker, or an interesting idea. If I had used the following two approaches earlier, I could have shaved time from my learning curve. Perhaps they will be helpful to you.

Quiet Your Mind When You Listen

Stan joined the table as the chicken was served. He'd been introduced to me earlier, and we'd talked briefly during the post-conference, pre-dinner social. Now he was peppering me with intriguing business questions. This was going to be a lively and interesting discussion, I thought.

My hopes vanished faster than an ice cube melting in the desert. I realized Stan wasn't listening. He didn't care what I had to say; he was waiting for his turn to talk. And talk he did, monopolizing the table's conversation with his back-patting soliloquy.

My expectations had been raised, believing that someone asking thoughtful questions might be interested in the answers. But that's a rare find in this too-busy-to-listen world. We're too busy answering cell phones, checking BlackBerries, and texting messages. We're so busy communicating that we fail to communicate. We think because we said something, it was understood. We confuse communicating with understanding, and silence with listening.

But the absence of talking is not necessarily listening. Real listening requires focused attention and a quiet mind. It's deep, not surface. You do it to understand, not so you can talk when someone pauses. Deep listening comes from the heart, as well as the head.

Deep listeners ignite ideas, influence outcomes, and build relationships. They're wonderful to be around. Few experiences in the workplace are more powerful than knowing someone is completely focused on what you're saying. It makes you feel valued and respected because what you have to say matters to them. Deep listeners create dialogues and enhance creativity. They also build their careers.

I learned to deepen my listening skills by using a technique called "reflective summary." For example, if I said to you, "I had a flat tire on the way to work and missed my boss's meeting," the typical response might be, "Yeah, I had a tough morning, too." Or you might share a similar experience. But a reflective summary statement summarizes your understanding of what was said. So you might respond, "You're concerned you missed your boss's meeting?" If you summarized my message correctly, then I'd continue with my concerns. If not, I'd clarify. Either way, we'd improve our communication.

You learn more by listening than talking, persuade more by understanding than arguing, and problem solve more by asking than telling. People who are *winning at working* have discovered the power of listening.

Stay Off the Path of Least Resistance
I spend a bit of time on airplanes. So I was surprised by what I observed on a regional jet. Yes, it was holiday travel. Yes, the flight was overbooked. Yes, infrequent and tired travelers were creating challenges for the only flight attendant. Still, she saw the small boy, no more than eight, seated in the exit row next to his grandfather. She chose to ignore him, wishing and hoping her safety message stating "a person must be over fifteen to sit in the exit row" would fix it. Maybe she didn't want the hassle of trying to reseat passengers on an already late flight. Maybe she was tired, too. Who knows?

What I do know is that despite the safety implications of her decision, she chose the path of least resistance that day. She's not alone. Many take that path at work. They choose the easier way rather than doing what needs to be done. But the path of least resistance leads away from *winning at working*.

You'll be on that path if you turn a blind eye to something you know needs to be solved but you don't want to "rock the boat"; or you let a mistake pass your desk for someone else to fix because it's too complicated; or you ignore a difficult person because you don't want to create conflict; or you pass off a poor performer to another department rather than face the difficult conversation; or you resolve the customer complaint without solving the bigger issue behind it.

In my thinking, that's the adult equivalent of my son, as a child, pretending he never noticed that the toilet paper roll needed to be replaced. He'd leave a sheet or two on the cardboard tube so he didn't have to be the one to do anything about it. Of course, no one in the house was fooled. No one at work is either.

The difference between doing the right thing and the easy thing significantly differentiates people's performance. We can debate what the right thing to do is at any time. Sometimes, it might be choosing the more difficult, time-consuming path or the one that comes with more risk. But like my son and that flight attendant, I think most of us know what the right thing is most of the time, and we know when we've chosen the easier way.

We can only offer the best of who we are, when we are connected to who we are. That connection evolves in multiple ways. A crucial one is understanding there are certain things we must do for ourselves if we want to bring our unique gifts to the world. Thinking is one.

Divergent viewpoints, power struggles, hierarchy, bureaucracy, politics, and personal interests all affect voices in the workplace. So how do you choose what's right? How do you differentiate messages? Whom do you listen to? My bottom-line advice echos Aristotle's: "The answer to the last appeal of what is right lies within a man's own heart. Trust yourself."

THE COURAGE TO ASK

The line between average and exceptional performance is dotted with ordinary behaviors. One such behavior is asking: asking what you don't know, need to know, or should be asking. Generally questions fall into four categories: information-based, request-based, personal-based, and can-of-worms-based. Here are examples of each.

- ★ *Information-based:* Why did my medical premium increase this year?
- ★ *Request-based:* To meet company objectives, may I hire a new programmer?
- ★ *Personal-based:* May I have Friday off?
- ★ *Can-of-worms-based:* How can we justify doing that when we promised we wouldn't?

Except in cases where the proverbial can-of-worms needs to be opened, most workplace asking may seem straightforward. Often, it's not. I was reminded of that when my husband was explaining to a nurse how he'd inadvertently taken the last dose of the live typhoid virus on the wrong day and wondered if he needed to retake the sequence prior to our Africa trip. "No," she commented, "I think you'll be fine." We both knew she was guessing.

While my husband was rolling down his sleeves after the set of immunizations, a different nurse poked her head into the room. "I overheard your conversation at the desk," she said to Dan. "We've never had that situation, so I thought it best to call the drug manufacturer for advice. Turns out you need to retake the entire dosage." We were grateful she decided to ask.

It's not possible to know all the answers to all the questions you'll get asked at work. So be willing to say when you don't. That's better than giving out misinformation or guessing at an answer without making it clear it's a guess. People who are *winning at working* add four words— "but I'll find out." And they do find out and get back to the person. That extra step differentiates their performance.

Jim was already in the department when I was hired to

manage it. "I don't know" was his typical response when queried beyond the surface status reports of his projects. At first, I expected him to automatically find out the answers to my questions and inform me, his new boss. But he never did. Jim managed to train me to follow-up his "I don't know" with "please find out and let me know."

Jim worked for me for two years, and at the time I moved on, I was still asking him to find out. For Jim and people like Jim, "I don't know" is a habitual way to reduce their task list. To them, "I don't know" ends it. What they don't realize is what else it ends in the minds of their bosses, clients, or customers.

It puzzles me that someone thinks saying "I don't know" suffices when it involves their work responsibilities. It baffles me how frequently people offer their best guesses as if they were factual answers. And it surprises me how few people take the small step to ask or find out. Those who do stand out. They go from guessing to knowing. Find out answers, and you'll build knowledge and credibility that differentiates you.

This kind of knowledge-based asking shouldn't take much courage. On a scale of workplace risk, it's a "1" at best. But if you're not comfortable asking the simple questions, moving up to asking the tougher ones will require a bit of courage.

REFLECTIVE ASSESSMENT EXERCISE:
ASSESS YOUR ASK-COURAGE

1 = Never 2 = Rarely 3 = Sometimes
4 = Usually 5 = Almost Always

1. Would you ask your boss for the resources you need to complete a significant company objective (i.e., staff, budget, time)?
2. Would you still ask if you'd been turned down on similar requests?
3. Would you ask to lead a project you were passionate about? (*continued on p. 38*)

(*continued from p. 37*)

4. Would you ask the knowledge-based question in a team meeting, the one that everyone had been talking about in the hallway before the meeting but no one had the courage to ask?
5. Would you ask your boss why you were passed over for promotion?
6. Would you ask for the big picture or the "why" behind a particular project you've been assigned?
7. Would you refrain from asking questions because you might look foolish?
8. Would you ask your boss, again, to explain something you're having trouble understanding?
9. Would you ask a teammate why she's clearly upset with you?
10. Would you take a risk for the good of the whole? That is, would you ask the question that opens the can-of-worms that needs opening?

Self-Reflective Scoring

If your total score is 35 or above, feel confident your ask-courage is thriving. If your total score is lower than 35, you may want to consider why asking is difficult for you. Then consider:

- *"He who asks is a fool for five minutes, but he who does not ask remains a fool forever."* Chinese Proverb

- *"Many things are lost for want of asking."* English Proverb

---

For half my career, I fell in the under-thirty-five, way-under, ask-courage category. I think of that time as my backwards-thinking period. I viewed the world from a self-absorbed perspective, worrying first how "I" might be perceived or judged if I were to ask something. My main concern was coming out ahead in a win (versus winning) strategy, and thus the reason behind any questions I asked—if I did ask them—was self-preservation or self-interest.

But when my orientation shifted to contribution over personal gain, my ask-courage soared and so did my asking results. Consider why you're asking. What's your motivation, intention, or purpose, especially when opening a can-of-worms? My asking experience is this: having a higher purpose yields more candid responses and affirmative answers. Differentiate when and how to ask the hard questions, ask for what is needed, and ask the questions others are fearful to ask. Bottom-line: ask for the right reasons, not to make yourself look good or someone else appear not as good.

THE COURAGE TO TELL

It's one thing to tell the truth when you're asked at work, and another to tell it when you're not, especially when personal risks are attached. But *hitting your stride* requires moments of courage. As Martin Luther King, Jr., said, "Our lives begin to end the day we become silent about things that matter."

While workplace issues pale next to larger societal ones, being naive to the soul-depleting impact of negative work cultures, ignoring damaging self-esteem verbal lashings, or pretending unethical or illegal practices will go away on their own is the choice many make, often out of fear. Fear that if they speak up, they'll lose their job, be labeled a troublemaker, or relegated to the "not promotable" category. Fear that is often justified.

Still, things are changing. I believe a revolution of the soul at work is quietly underway. When you offer the best of who you are to the workplace—and thousands and millions of other people do the same—a path to change emerges. Slow. Steady. Uphill certainly. But if we accept nothing less from ourselves, we contribute to a vision of a workplace future where kindness, love, compassion, understanding, and integrity maximize profits and actualize human potential.

Today, that's a "big audacious hairy" dream, but tomorrow's children will expect nothing less. These soulful companies of the future, and the people who blaze the way for them, need both courage and vision. If you're reading this book, it's likely you're one of these pioneers.

Courage comes from mental or moral strength. Motivational speaker Brian Tracy puts it this way: "Courage combined with integrity is the foundation of character. The first form of courage is your ability to stick to your principles, to stand for what you believe in and to refuse to budge unless you feel right about the alternative." Yet we're often told by bosses and co-workers to "go along to get along," "don't rock the boat," "don't make waves," or "it's not a hill to die on."

The truth is—it may not be a hill to die on. There are risks and there are rewards when speaking truth to power. I've experienced both. Naively believing that the senior vice president asking my opinion actually wanted it, I gave him the truth. At least the "truth" as I knew it from working with people in the field, and the truth I saw from my role-perspective. Thinking I was doing my job, I was honest about why I disagreed with his recommendation and even debated his perspective. The next day, my boss's boss called me to her office to inform me I had "overstepped" my bounds, "didn't know my place," and was being transferred to another SVP's area at his request. Gulp!

Years later, when asked to write a white paper for a new company president on a problematic issue, I hesitated. Haunted by the earlier experience, I was afraid. How honest could I be without risking my job or affecting my career? It took me two days to write the paper and two weeks to find the courage to offer him my well-intentioned, tell-it-like-I-saw-it input.

I believe the words we silence, the half-truths we propagate, the stories we spin, the fear we let encase us, damages our spirit and compromises our soul. So I concluded I was willing to risk my job but not my *self*. I wrote the white paper from my heart because it was important for me and my self-respect. Not doing so would have compromised who I was, what I stood for, and what I believed. Realizing that left me no alternative.

The good news is I didn't get fired. In fact, unimagined opportunities emerged as a result. However, I would be remiss if I didn't offer a warning through that idealism.

Backbiting, infighting, and deceitfulness do exist, and there are likely as many people who would like to see you fail as succeed. Kahlid Hossein's protagonist crystallizes it in *The Kite Runner* when he says, "And that's the thing about people who mean everything they say. They think everyone else does, too."

Ultimately the decision to speak from your heart can be difficult since most issues are hardly black or white. Only you can determine whether, in the scheme of things, it matters. Not all hills are worth dying on, so here are a few questions you might want to consider.

REFLECTIVE ASSESSMENT EXERCISE:
IN THE SCHEME OF THINGS ... DOES IT MATTER?

- Can you look yourself in the eye, knowing you offered the best of who you are to the world if you *don't* say what you feel needs to be said? If you do say it?
- In a month or a year, will this issue matter? To you? To the company?
- What do you hope to achieve by telling? What is your motivation? If there's a personal agenda, extra caution is required.
- Is there something gnawing at you? What's that about?
- What would you want if the situation were reversed?
- What do you fear by speaking up? By being silent?
- Are you willing to risk your job if it comes to that?

The Emperor's New Clothes was a favorite childhood story. I couldn't believe all those adults standing around, watching the emperor make a fool of himself, and not telling him the truth. When I grew up and went to work, I discovered it wasn't that easy. What do you say when the boss asks you to comment on her work, and it's not so hot? How do you offer a contrary viewpoint in a room full of aligned people?

My experience confirms there are emperor's ministers alive and well in today's workplace. Ask a staff member what she thinks, and it's likely she's more concerned with figuring out what she thinks her boss wants to hear. Too often, people are more concerned about looking foolish, than venturing feedback; more concerned with what they think they should say, than saying what needs to be said; and more concerned with going along, than offering their point of view. Fortunately, there are exceptions.

I never would have succeeded if others hadn't stopped me from being like the emperor in the children's fable. I sought inner-circle people for my staff who were willing to push back, challenge, offer opinions, and tell me things I may not have wanted, but needed, to hear. Now as a writer and speaker, my criterion remains the same. I need people to tell me what needs telling, whether I ask for it or not. Everyone does.

Sure I may not always like what they have to say, but I'm glad they said it. I may not always take their advice, but I appreciate that they offered it. And I may not always agree with them, but I know to listen deeply and consider it. I've been saved from countless mistakes and blind spots by these exceptional people offering their opinions and truth-telling gifts. They've helped me keep my balance, gain perspective, and make decisions.

"Your idea is way off base," a teammate said. "It's not going to connect with people." These words from this trusted colleague cautioned me to rethink an important launch. In the end, she was right. It wasn't a good idea. Her words saved me from the certain embarrassment of a failed initiative. Money, resources, and time were at stake, too.

If you want to be *winning at working*, look for people like this to help you. You'll know them from their candor. They're the ones who are not working a personal agenda, but instead have the company's best interests at heart; the ones able to see the big picture; the ones comfortable offering their no-strings-attached perspectives. They're the ones telling you the truth as they see it, who are willing to pull you back from the edge. I'm indebted to these people in my career.

My suggestion? Realize you need all the help you can

get if you want to be *winning at working*. Find a few truth-telling people you can trust. I look for people who have courage and forthrightness, like the child in Hans Christian Andersen's, *The Emperor's New Clothes*. If I'm out there without my clothes on, it's a sure bet I want someone to tell me.

There's a second part to that equation. Return the favor. I would never have had the opportunities I did if I wasn't able to find the courage, at appropriate times, to speak up. Don't get me wrong here. This is not the "diarrhea of the mouth" some people call "being honest," in which hurtful intent damages more than careers. Rather, it's what I learned the hard way: when you speak from the heart, with an honorable purpose, people want to listen.

The courage to tell boils down to moral courage and self-trust. I like British Field Marshal William Slim's definition: "Moral courage simply means you do what you think is right without bothering too much about the effect on yourself." When I was young and idealistic, I thought that was easy. Now I understand the complexity of seemingly simple things and know how difficult it can be to always meet that definition. But I know one thing—I like myself better when I do.

THE COURAGE TO LEAVE

Once there was a young woman who didn't like her job. Everyday when she came home from work, she told her husband how terrible her day had been, how tiring the work, and how unreasonable her boss.

"Leave that job," her husband told her.

"Oh, I will," she said. "But not yet. I have too many friends there for me to leave just yet."

And so it went until the days became years, and her family grew to five.

"Leave that job," her children told her.

"Oh, I will," she said. "But not yet. I have seniority and four weeks vacation. I'm not ready to start over just yet.

And so it went until the years became decades, and her children had children.

"Leave that job," her grandchildren told her.

"Oh, I will," she said. "But not yet. There's only seven more years until I reach thirty years of service and can retire. So I can't just yet."

I know this woman. And scores like her. People who settle for where they are, what they're doing, and how they're doing it. People who have planted their feet in status-quo cement, lacking the courage to move from what is to what could be. People experiencing work like a four-letter word and doing nothing to change it.

They remind me of the story about an old dog half-asleep on the porch of the general store, moaning and groaning in the sun. "Why is your dog acting that way?" a customer asked the store owner.

"Oh," answered the man, "he's lying on a nail."

"Well, why doesn't he move?"

"Because it's not hurting him bad enough."

That's true for people, too. We convince ourselves the pain is not bad enough to leave. But we're wrong.

Work pain is damaging. Some damages our self-esteem, kills our passion, or destroys our dreams. Some emerges when we compromise our values, quiet our voice, or hide our talent. Some happens when we're seduced by power or believe our own myths of importance and significance. Some occurs when we look the other way, say "yes" when we mean "no," or forfeit the promises we made to ourselves. And some eats away at our future by hampering our learning, growing, and thinking. Pain at work prohibits us from offering the best of who we are. It also prohibits us from sharing our gifts and passion at work.

Wilbur Wright, of the Wright Brothers' fame, once commented, "We could hardly wait to get up in the morning." I know that exhilarating feeling of being so passionate about something I was working on that I couldn't wait to get back to work. In *The World According to Mister Rogers*, Fred Rogers comments, "The thing I remember best about successful people I've met all through the years is their obvious delight in what they're doing . . . and it seems to have very little to do with worldly success. They just love

REFLECTIVE ASSESSMENT EXERCISE:
DO YOU HAVE PASSION IN YOUR JOB?

If the statement below is more true than false for you—choose true (T)

If the statement below is more false than true for you—choose false (F)

1. My work is more than a paycheck to me. T F
2. Getting a new project mostly means getting extra work. T F
3. I can't remember the last time I felt excited about work. T F
4. I find my mood negatively shifting as Monday approaches. T F
5. I feel like a passenger in my work life. T F
6. My fuse is short regarding changes and problems at work. T F
7. I am a frequent contributor of ideas and suggestions at work. T F
8. I volunteer for projects and new assignments. T F
9. My knowledge and skills continue to grow at work. T F
10. Work feels like work. T F
11. The work day goes by quickly. T F
12. People come to me for help and input. T F
13. No one notices what I do or how hard I work. T F
14. I work extra because I want to. T F
15. I'm bored at work most days. T F
16. Clients, customers, and/or co-workers often annoy me. T F
17. Work is like a good hobby—interesting and fun. T F
18. I like to learn new things at work. T F
19. I keep an updated resume and an eye out for something better. T F
20. My unique gifts and abilities are utilized in my work. T F
21. I often feel burned-out and disillusioned around work. T F
22. I get excited when I talk about what I do. T F

(continued on p. 46)

(*continued from p. 45*)
23. If I could leave my job, I would. T F
24. I'm proud of what I do. T F
25. Most people who know me know I like what I do. T F

Self-Reflective Scoring
Count the number of Ts you marked for each of these thirteen questions: 1, 7, 8, 9, 11, 12, 14, 17, 18, 20, 22, 24, and 25. If your total is 10 or more, more often than not, you find passion in your job. If your score is below 10, this section may give you a few ideas for changing your direction. I've found the 51 percent rule helpful. If on average, I enjoy what I'm doing more than 51 percent of the time, I like my job.

what they're doing, and they love it in front of others." Unfortunately, many of us don't have that kind of work passion.

I wish the media had heralded the *Conference Board* statistics saying half of Americans are satisfied with their job. Meaning, of course, half are dissatisfied. When more than half of Americans were identified as overweight, major news outlets began educating us on how to stay out, or get out, of that statistic. But disliking your job is hazardous to your health and well-being, too. You can't be *hitting your stride* if you're dissatisfied with your work or languishing in the status quo of dislike.

Spending the majority of your waking hours dissatisfied, like being overweight, depletes your energy and kidnaps your spirit. You can change all that. And looking for a new job should not be where you start. At least not yet.

First, consider what is causing your dissatisfaction. Maybe it's that annoying co-worker or irritating boss that's holding you back. Maybe if you only made more money. Maybe the work's boring or the company's unfair. Whatever your reasons, pause your thinking and go to step two: look deeper. More than likely, what's at the root of your dissatisfaction are your doubts, fears, and insecurities.

Too often, we become victims in our own life. We blame McDonald's for having french fries that make us fat, and blame bosses who give us substandard raises, when in fact, we control whether the french fries gets purchased and put in our mouth, or we do the quality of work that meets the performance standards for a higher raise. It's a choice. And choices bring accountability. It's easier to believe we're a victim of circumstances than a driver of our own future. But this easier choice comes at a price: dissatisfaction.

The harder choice comes with a price too: personal accountability. That means when you're running an obstacle course and discover you're the obstacle, you correct your thinking, enhance your skills, and persist through your fears. It means, if you don't get the raise, the promotion, or the more interesting work, you look in the mirror first.

Sure, in the end, you may determine you need to change jobs or environments. Just be certain it's the job you're dissatisfied with, or you may find the same irritating co-workers and unfair bosses, with different names of course, waiting for you in the new job.

People who are *winning at working* don't see themselves as victims. They know the choices they make have consequences and payoffs. While fears, self-doubts, and insecurities may stall their progress, challenge their courage, and test their persistence, it doesn't stop them.

It's not easy to move through your fears, build your self-esteem, or change your negative self-talk. But few things in life worth having are easy. People who are *winning at working* do the hard self-work. They're unwilling to let their fears, doubts and insecurities orchestrate the outcome of their lives, at work or at home. To them, the biggest dissatisfaction would be wondering about the person they *could* have been.

Not all corporate cultures work for all people, and stifled voices lose their passion at work. Finding an environment where you can thrive requires work, persistence, and self-understanding. It also may require the courage to leave. But keep in mind that the best environment may not be in another company, but another department or another role.

Ultimately if we don't want to be blowing in the wind, we're challenged to become who we are capable of becoming.

Isn't that why we're here? To make a difference somehow by being who we are?

It seems to me, being yourself is your life's responsibility and your biggest contributions come when you are able to be yourself. Nobel Peace Prize winner and former UN Secretary General Dag Hammarskjöld said, "What you must dare is to be yourself." But that takes courage. The courage to find and use your voice, think for yourself, ask the difficult questions, offer your wisdom, speak from your heart, and leave an environment that blocks your gifts.

I chose to use the word "courage" for this section because most workplaces are not yet aligned with well-intentioned, best-of-who-you-are approaches that are also devoid of negative politics and personal gain. It takes courage to find and use your voice when others around you aren't. And it can be very lonely. But the more we connect with the best of who we are and offer our uniqueness at work, embracing that approach in ourselves and others, the more our outside world will become transformed.

Let me leave you with this thought from Theodor Geisel, a.k.a. Dr. Seuss: "Be who you are and say what you feel 'cause people who mind don't matter and people who matter don't mind."

3

Seeing the Elephant

"What we think or what we know or what we believe is, in the end, of little consequence. The only consequence is what we do." **John Ruskin**

The Blind Men and the Elephant . . .
By John Godfrey Saxe

It was six men of Indostan
To learning much inclined,
Who went to see the Elephant
(Though all of them were blind),
That each by observation
Might satisfy his mind.

The First approached the Elephant,
And, happening to fall
Against his broad and sturdy side,
At once began to bawl:
"God bless me! but the Elephant,
Is nothing but a wall!"

The Second, feeling of the tusk,
Cried: "Ho! What have we here
So very round and smooth and sharp?
To me 'tis mighty clear
This wonder of an Elephant
Is very like a spear!"

The Third approached the animal,
And, happening to take
The squirming trunk within his hands,
Thus boldly up and spake:
"I see," quoth he, "The Elephant
Is very like a snake!"

The Fourth reached out his eager hand,
And felt about the knee:
"What most this wondrous beast is like
Is mighty plain," quoth he;
"Tis clear enough the Elephant
Is very like a tree!"

The Fifth who chanced to touch the ear,
Said: "E'en the blindest man
Can tell what this resembles most:
Deny the fact who can,
This marvel of an Elephant
Is very like a fan!"

The Sixth no sooner had begun
About the beast to grope
Than seizing on the swinging tail
That fell within his scope,
"I see," quoth he, "the Elephant
Is very like a rope!"

And so these men of Indostan
Disputed loud and long.
Each in his own opinion
Exceeding stiff and strong,
Though each was partly in the right,
And all were in the wrong!

Moral:
So, oft in theologic wars
The disputants, I ween,
Rail on in utter ignorance

Of what each other mean,
And prate about an Elephant
No one of them has seen!

L ike the story of the blind men trying to picture what
an elephant looks like, finding the tail and thinking
it's like a rope, or finding a leg and thinking it's like a tree,
I've made plenty of wrong assumptions from correct information. I've believed with certainty in my direction only
to discover I was following the wrong map. And I've taken
detours by holding on to misguided understandings.

I've learned the hard way that what I think I know may
not be right. At times, I've been as blind as those men in
John Godfrey Saxe's poem. That blindness significantly affected my ability to be *winning at working*. I know firsthand that limited perspective limits results.

Thinking itself the "western-most point of civilization,"
Spain had as part of its coat of arms, the motto "*ne plus
ultra*," nothing more beyond. We're like fifteenth-century
Spain, believing that how we see our piece of the work
world *is* the world. But it's not. Spain learned that lesson
in 1493 when Columbus returned, making their motto
obsolete. Queen Isabella removed the "*ne*" changing it to
"*plus ultra*," or *more beyond*. That's good thinking for our
changing work world, too.

Now in the first decade of the twenty-first century, NASA
photographs of space—such as the "Steep Cliffs of Mars,"
the "Fox Fur Nebula," and "Markarians Chain of Galax-
ies"—hint at what "more beyond" might mean for our
world five centuries after Columbus. Wireless technologies, virtual workplaces, and a worldwide 24/7 marketplace
leave "more beyond" hints in the workplace as well.

Developing a "more beyond" perspective within a
greater context, aligning with an organization's vision, values, and objectives, and growing "new eyes" to help differentiate results is what this chapter is about.

THE BIG TEAM

Engrossed in a book, I hardly noticed the only person seated across the emergency exit row aisle from me on a regional jet. When approached by the flight attendant, we both agreed to follow the prescribed safety requirements associated with our better-legroom seats. So it surprised me when I noticed him sitting sideways across two seats during takeoff, clearly not wearing his seatbelt. Instantly, I thought, "how foolish." That was immediately followed by the thought—"how irresponsible." What if there had been an emergency, and he'd been thrown from his seat and blocked the exit?

"Idiot" crossed my mind next. The word is from the Greek "idios," meaning "one's own private affairs." To be an idiot in ancient Greece was to be someone who "ignored the health and security of the whole in order to manage his own affairs." That's a good description of my fellow passenger, oblivious to the impact his action could have had on fifty people. He was on a team of one.

Mao Tse-Tung put it this way: "We think too small. Like the frog at the bottom of the well. He thinks the sky is only as big as the top of the well. If he surfaced, he would have an entirely different view."

Understanding and applying Big Team concepts requires us to surface from our well of small thinking to look out at this world we share. When we do, we realize it's a very Big Team out there. And that changes everything.

I'm not going to kid you. Making decisions for the greater good is not common workplace behavior. And the concepts in this chapter are beyond the considerations of many who see winning as the opposite of losing. I contend those people are playing the wrong game. There's a bigger one, and in the Big Team scheme of things, we only win when we're all winning.

What we're able to see, choose to see, or learn to see— literally or figuratively—affects our perspective, our understanding, and our results. Last time I was hiking in Montana's Glacier National Park, I stopped to view, through binoculars, a mountain goat trekking atop a rock cliff. My husband, viewing the switchback trail we'd just climbed, happened to see a grizzly bear cross behind a group of hikers a hundred yards below us. With my narrowed focus, I never saw the bear. Our different perspectives yielded different impressions.

It's like that at work, too. We survey our landscape using departmental binoculars, seeing the elephant through lenses of a work group, a site, a division, a subsidiary, or a corporation. We may see the goat and miss the bear, or vice versa. We then make decisions, offer solutions, create ideas, and do our work based on the understanding we've gleaned.

Whether you're in software development or human resources, customer service or accounting, sales or creative services, manufacturing or marketing, legal or public relations, or any number of departments or businesses, you'll tend to see your work world from your role perspective and interpret the elephant with a lens particular to that orientation.

Looking beyond your little team helps you to grow bigger team eyes. But the Big Team has nothing to do with larger numbers of people or the size of a department or a company or a business enterprise. It has nothing to do with where you are in the hierarchy. People with myopic self-interests can be found at every level of an organization. It's not the position that helps us see, it's the "eyes" we develop.

The Big Team is an orientation, a mindset, a way of thinking. It's understanding one overriding concept: we are not separate. We're interconnected. Actions by one person affect another person. Actions in one department affect another department. Actions in one business affect another business. Actions in one industry affect another industry. Actions in one country affect another country.

Let's say, for example, you implement a change from paper to electronic invoices. That decision affects the printer of the paper invoices, the shipper of the forms, the IT department needing to build new electronic systems, suppliers who must adapt to your way of doing business, employees who must be trained on the electronic system, and . . . you get the point. Knowing the impact doesn't mean you won't make the change. But it enables you to antici-pate and manage more positive results.

When you think beyond your little team to all stake-holders, you're on the Big Team. When you consider the common good, you're on the Big Team. And when you step back, reviewing the impact of what you're doing, you step into the Big Team. Do that enough, and you grow "new eyes" and see more of the elephant. But I know from per-sonal experience, it's easier said than done. Like the de-velopment of any skill, developing Big Team thinking in-volves practice.

Once at a company retreat, a group of senior leaders, me included, competitively hunkered down to win the Broken Squares game as if our annual earnings depended on the result. Seated at tables in small groups, we were instructed how to win the game: assemble a square in front of each person using five puzzle pieces. The rules were straightforward. We had to assemble our own square; we couldn't talk during the process; we couldn't take pieces from another player even if that piece would complete our square; and pieces could be offered by the player who "owned" them.

Clues to solving the problem, provided verbally by the facilitator, were repeated several times as our progress waned. It was a long, frustrating exercise. Some thought they'd won the game when their square was finished, so they stopped participating. Some thought they'd won when each person at their table completed a square and likewise stopped being involved.

It turned out winning occurred only when everyone in the room had a completed square in front of them. But for that to happen, some people with finished squares needed to break theirs apart and offer their pieces to others. In-stead, we tended to protect our finished squares. Stuck in silo thinking, we never won. The lack of Big Team thinking caused us to fail miserably at the task.

It was an interesting exercise, mirroring behaviors back in the office and highlighting improvements needed. I took it as a developmental challenge. So instead of thinking the decisions I made were confined within the invisible walls of responsibility, I tried to step back and consider the impact on other departments and stakeholders.

I even considered I might be holding the equivalent of a puzzle piece that I needed to offer the Big Team—like the time I initiated moving one of my favorite start-up projects and an important company initiative to another vice president because I believed I was no longer the right person to take it to the next level. It was a difficult decision since I was passionate about the area. But it was the right Big Team decision.

Big Team thinking requires a balance between intrapersonal and interpersonal interests. It uses analytical, practical, and creative abilities to discern the bigger playing field. It means working for the greater good of the whole. Here are two examples snatched from the headlines:

* Flu vaccination shortage. Over sixteen million Americans gave up getting a flu shot so those more in need were protected.
* International outpouring of aid following the Indonesia tsunami that killed over three hundred thousand people.

Some of you may be saying, "wait a minute." It's one thing to work for the greater good of the whole during natural disasters or a national crisis, but how practical is that for the workplace? Aren't we supposed to compete with each other at work so we can win the promotion or raise? There are only so many pieces to the company pie after all, right?

Wrong. Growing the Big Team mindset shifts the competition from out-there with others to in-here with self. If you're on the Big Team, the objective is not competition with teammates. You're on the same team, remember. The objective is to help the Big Team by creating a bigger pie so everyone can have a piece, or a bigger piece. That's winning. Your part is to compete with yourself, incrementally developing your skills and talents so you can offer the best "you" to the Big Team.

HOW BIG?

The story goes that on a large sheet of paper tacked up on the conference room wall, the consultant placed a small black circle. "What do you see?" he asked each person in the group. He'd been hired to help improve their businesses during the 1930's depression. Each man's answer was the same. "I see a black dot."

Pausing to get their attention he responded, "Yes, there is a black dot. But none of you saw the big sheet of paper. You didn't concentrate on the whole picture, just the little spot. That's my advice to you on how you can go about improving your businesses."

And that's my advice to you on how you can go about improving your *winning at working* skills. Concentrate on the whole picture. Here are a few examples:

★ Jennifer knew the right decision for her department was to fire Matthew, a poor-performing teammate who was unable to handle his share of the work. But she also knew it wasn't the best decision for the company to fire a long-serviced staff member, a beloved community volunteer, and a noted local commissioner. Her solution—Jennifer worked persistently for eight months to get Matthew assigned to community affairs where his skills were an asset.

★ "It's not my job." Ever heard that? Ever think it? In the context of the small team or work group, you may be right to think it's not in your job description. But there's a bigger context: what needs to be done for the common good of building a company. That's everyone's job. If you were the owner, you'd do whatever it took to build your business. Thinking like one goes beyond the small dot of a defined role.

★ In *Miracle on 34th Street,* Macy's controversial Santa informs customers where to find the items their children want for Christmas, even sending them to other stores. Customers are so grateful to Macy's for locating sought-after items that it makes the news. Soon, competitor Gimbels mimics the approach. This takes Macy's and Gimbels away from their "small dots" of store purchases to the "bigger paper" of customer satisfaction. Santa's view is even larger—making kids' wishes come true.

How big is the space beyond your black dot and the paper's edge? Thinking from larger and larger vantage points takes practice and focus. So does considering and balancing stakeholder interests. Improve yours by consciously thinking about the Big Team and applying these:

Ten Tips for Increasing Your Perspective

1. Perspective starts with thoughts, and you're in charge of yours. How big you make your Big Team is up to you. Think of it like lifting weights. When you start, ten pounds may feel right, but eventually you'll need twelve or fifteen or twenty pounds to keep building muscle. Growing your perspective requires mental weight lifting.
2. When you think you're seeing the elephant, assume you're not. As Spain discovered, there's more beyond. Keep asking, "What more is beyond what I'm seeing now? What's beyond that?"
3. Draw your own conclusions. Ever look for pictures in the clouds? Sometimes you could see the ones your friend found, and sometimes you couldn't, or vice versa. Remember, we don't have the same experiences, understanding, or knowledge.
4. Take yourself out of the picture. You can't see the elephant when you're looking in the mirror.
5. Identify stakeholders. Then consider the situation and impact from the vantage point of each.
6. Watch for connections. Notice how each action, person, or event influences another. Step outside

yourself, and notice what you're affecting with your actions.

7. Know yourself, including biases, filters, and lenses. As philosopher Henri Bergson reminds us, "The eye sees only what the mind is prepared to comprehend."

8. Once you determine the best decision for your work group, consider the best decision for your department, then for the company. Sometimes they're the same, but not always. Go with what's best for the company.

9. Consider the common good of the whole. Define what that means in the current situation.

10. Ask yourself, "In the scheme of what *really* matters, how important is this?" Proceed accordingly.

When my son was a toddler and learning to talk, he'd respond to the question, "How big are you?" by first laughing, then throwing his arms over his head and declaring proudly, "So big!" The exercise below is a little like that. You can see for yourself "how big" your thinking might be. Try it again in three months, then in six, and note the difference.

REFLECTIVE THINKING EXERCISE: HOW BIG?

Read each situation and write down the one response most typical of you. Compare your answers with the key, adding or subtracting the points to get your "How Big" score.

Consider the following:

1. Your division met its goals. Another division hasn't. They have openings they haven't been able to fill. Processing is behind, and it's starting to affect customers. You receive an e-mail from the vice president of that area asking for volunteers to help out nights or weekends to catch up.

   a. You read the e-mail and delete it.

  b. You read it, consider it, but don't respond.

  c. You call the VP to get more information.

  d. You send the e-mail to your staff.

  e. You volunteer to help on two Saturdays.

2. You have letters that must go out today, and you didn't have time to go to the post office on your way to work. You:

  a. Use the company's postage meter.

  b. Go out at lunch and buy stamps.

3. Your company is having a community-service event, and you've signed up to participate. You figure it's nice to do, but it doesn't hurt to get noticed by the "powers that be" who will be there. The day before the event, you discover your vice president and the company's president won't be attending. You:

  a. Attend anyway.

  b. Show up briefly, then offer an excuse and leave.

  c. Decide there's no reason to go.

4. You've been called to a meeting with your boss and his boss. They're looking for input on a potential project with significant cost implications. You have expertise on its technical aspects. You know your boss supports the idea, but you've expressed reservations to him before about the huge technical challenges. His boss is asking for your opinion. You:

  a. Go with what you know your boss wants.

  b. Walk the middle, offering pros and cons.

  c. Offer your honest opinion.

5. The department head of the international division contacts you. She's in need of expertise, and there's someone in your department who has it. Turns out she wants to recruit Chad, your star employee, for a new venture. You know it's a good opportunity for him, but you can't afford to give him up since your department has no bench strength. You agree to talk to Chad, and you:

  a. Present the opportunity factually and fairly, realizing your star needs to make his own decision.

  b. Present the opportunity in a way to try to influence his decision to stay in your department.

(*continued on p. 60*)

(*continued from p. 59*)

6. It's budget preparation time, and you're new to the company. You check around and hear that budgets are routinely cut 10 to 20 percent. On the basis of that information you:
    a. Pad your budget submission 20 percent so when it gets cut, you'll get the budget you want.
    b. Submit the budget you need with a wish list identified.
    c. Align your budget with company goals and objectives.

7. You come in on Saturday and find a group of employees working in a back part of the office. It's clear, based on the pungent odor and scattered beer bottles, they've been doing something other than working. One of them comes to you and asks you not to say anything. You:
    a. Don't want to rock the boat so you tell her you won't.
    b. Tell her you can't do that and make the appropriate call.

8. Management has been shuffled and direction has changed. You've been told you must cut two members of your team. Your new boss wants one person he personally dislikes on the cut list. The person is a strong contributor. You:
    a. Don't make waves and do what's asked.
    b. Try to convince your boss he's wrong about her.
    c. Develop a profile of your team, with individual strengths, weaknesses, contributions, and rankings. When you discuss it with your boss, you make a request to keep her and offer to take accountability for the decision.

9. The company you work for is struggling. During the two years you've been there, they've been generous and fair. This is a first for financial problems. There are several potential contracts to be signed in the next nine months. Rather than face layoffs, the CEO is asking employees to take a voluntary pay cut of 10 percent for no more than one year, assuring everyone they'll receive their money with interest as soon as the contracts are in. You:
    a. Figure it's not your fault the company is in a mess—

it's management's. You decide not to volunteer.

b. Decide it's time to look for another job and don't volunteer.

c. Know your finances will be tight, but volunteer anyway.

10. A peer supervisor is struggling in his performance and asks you for help, input, and coaching. You:

a. Tell him you'd love to but just don't have the time.

b. Reluctantly agree, giving him general feedback and comments.

c. Agree and do everything you can to help him, offering honest, productive feedback, as well as sharing tips and insights.

11. You have a great idea for a new product that is uniquely right for your company. You:

a. Decide it's too good an idea to share.

b. Champion it and make it happen.

c. Share the idea with others who might champion it.

12. You are aware of a particular situation that could be harmful to your company. You're not sure whether or not to speak up. You're concerned if you do it might affect your career. You decide to:

a. Tell your boss and hope that she will do the right thing.

b. Share the information with a trusted friend at work.

c. Be quiet and not risk your career.

d. Tell the people who should know.

13. You are in a team meeting. Your manager is looking for input, but everyone is reluctant to speak up. They're skimming over the problems that are jeopardizing a deadline. You:

a. Don't think it's your place to speak up either.

b. Send the manager an e-mail after the meeting with issues.

c. Speak up and identify concerns.

14. At lunch, the latest corporate rumor is all the buzz in the cafeteria, and people are concerned. It's occupying everyone's time. You:

a. Repeat the rumor to co-workers in the afternoon.

(*continued on p. 62*)

(continued from p. 61)

    b. Offer perspective that it's only a rumor.

    c. Ask your boss about it after lunch.

    d. Help kill the rumor once you have truthful information.

15. You have several personal business tasks to take care of that you can't do on a Saturday. You need a day off to get everything done. You:

    a. Call in sick.

    b. Request and schedule a vacation day.

SCORING FOR "HOW BIG" EXERCISE

Add or subtract the number next to the answer you chose, and then total your score.

1.	a = 0	b = 0	c = 1	d = 1	e = 2
2.	a = -1	b = 1			
3.	a = 1	b = 0	c = -1		
4.	a = 0	b = 1	c = 2		
5.	a = 2	b = 0			
6.	a = 0	b = 1	c = 2		
7.	a = -1	b = 2			
8.	a = 0	b = 1	c = 2		
9.	a = 0	b = 1	c = 2		
10.	a = 0	b = 1	c = 2		
11.	a = 0	b = 2	c = 1		
12.	a = 1	b = 0	c = 0	d = 2	
13.	a = 0	b = 1	c = 2		
14.	a = -1	b = 1	c = 1	d = 2	
15.	a = -1	b = 1			

Self-Reflection Scoring

If your total score is 18 or above, feel confident you're considering the impact of your actions on a bigger team. If your total score is less than 18, use the information for self-feedback and coaching. Review "Ten Tips for Increasing Your Perspective."

CONNECTING THE DOTS

Developing a Big Team mindset is step one in seeing the elephant. Step two is connecting the dots by linking mindset with actions. Three of my favorite ways to do that include:

* ★ Defining your purpose
* ★ Changing your language
* ★ Aligning your actions

Like childhood workbooks where connecting the dots illuminates the picture hidden within the page, you can increase your ability to see the big picture, i.e., the elephant. Connecting the right dots at work will bring the elephant's outline into view. But climbing higher in an organization doesn't automatically give you the Big Team perspective, help you connect the dots, or see the elephant. It's not our vantage point but our skill set that helps us "see."

Increasing your perspective increases your results. Once you find and see the elephant, you'll look for and see other elephants more easily. You'll see things you couldn't see before. It's the difference between thinking you know what it's like to be a parent and realizing how limited your previous thinking was once you became one. Supreme Court Justice Oliver Wendell Holmes, Jr., put it this way: "The mind, once expanded to the dimensions of larger ideas, never returns to its original size."

1. Defining Your Purpose

You increase your big-picture perspective when you define your work within the context of your organization's vision, values, goals, and objectives. Also, there's a good chance you'll find increased work satisfaction when you do. Why? Most of us want to know that what we're doing matters. So when you begin to understand your work in the context of the larger whole, you're better able to see how your work does matter.

Have you heard the story of the two masons working side by side at a building site? They're doing the same work under pretty much the same conditions. Then one day, a stranger comes along, approaches one of the men, and asks him, "What are you doing?"

"I don't know and I don't care," replies the man, his voice brimming with irritation. All I do is slap this crummy mortar on these crummy bricks and pile them up in a crummy line. That's what I'm doing."

The stranger returns to the building site the following day. This time he approaches the second man, asking him the same question. "Tell me," he said, "what are you doing?" Smiling at the stranger, the man proudly replies, "Why, I'm helping to build the new cathedral." The second mason saw a defined purpose in his work.

What are you helping to build in your workplace? Why does your work matter? Before you say it doesn't, think again. You have a role on the Big Team, and that role is important or you wouldn't be paid to do it. Of course, it's unlikely you'll find the purpose outlined in your job description. That's because defining your purpose is not in the tasks you do. It's in the reason for the tasks.

So if you're an employment specialist in human resources, your purpose is not to hire people. That's a task. The reason behind the task might be to increase your company's competitive edge with exceptional people. If you're a web designer, your job is not to build websites. That's a task. Your purpose is in the "why" of it. Maybe it's to build the corporate brand or make life easier for your customers. In one of my jobs, my purpose was to help the company develop a winning culture; in another it was to help build trust in the corporate brand so new customers would give us a try. My job title would never have told you about either. Look beyond your title.

Until you define and articulate your purpose at work and align that purpose with your organization's vision, values, goals, and objectives, you'll be like the first mason in the story, doing tasks without understanding why they matter. You won't be able to see the big picture. It's when we've defined our purpose and know how we contribute to the whole that we start connecting the dots, glimpsing the elephant, and discovering our work.

2. Changing Your Language

Your words can stop you from ever seeing the elephant. I'm not referring to caustic ones spoken or received, with sarcasm, irritation, anger, or frustration, carrying an emotional punch. I'm talking about simple, everyday, normal word choices. These words, like black ice, are not an obvious danger at first glance. But words can tether your view at a twelve-hundred-foot level instead of allowing you to climb to the view at thirty thousand feet or higher. So—user beware.

Words create impressions, images, and expectations. They build psychological connections. They influence how we think. And since thoughts determine actions, there's a powerful connection between the words you use, the elephant you think you see, and the results you get.

Think about these two words: spend and invest. Would you like your bank to spend your money or invest it? Since spending implies the money is gone, you probably want a bank that invests. Now apply these same words to corporate budgets and see how that influences your thinking.

Early in my career, I saw budgets as allocated company money I had permission to spend. And I did spend it. I never thought of budgets as investing in the company's future until I was given profit-and-loss accountability for a new department and discovered my flawed thinking. I learned that in order to grow the department, I needed to budget with an investment mentality. Shifting words shifted my thinking, my perspective, and my results.

Try these words: problem and challenge. Would you rather a boss see your mistake as a problem or as a challenge? It's more than semantics. Problems are fixed; challenges are met. Different words evoke different feelings. I have a more positive frame of mind meeting a challenge than fixing a problem. But a word of caution—I'm not suggesting you play the buzzword game like a colleague of mine who walked into my office saying, "Do I have an opportunity for you." We both knew differently.

Here are two favorites: bodies and people. As a young manager, I was jolted every time I heard another manager talking about how many "bodies" they needed, or putting "butts in seats." Later, I learned many of those managers struggled with departmental morale problems. I could understand why if their perspective on people was as interchangeable pieces to a puzzle rather than as individuals playing an important role in their departments.

I realized that the words I use to think and talk about my workload, my goals, my projects, and the people I work with influence my thoughts and actions about them. So I've changed my words. If I say I work "for" someone, I have a different vision about my work life than if I work "with" them; same with my staff working with, not for me.

Poorly chosen words can limit your perspective and stop you from ever seeing the elephant. They can kill enthusiasm, affect self-esteem, lower expectations, and hold you back. Well-chosen ones can help connect the dots, create vision, and move you forward. Learn to change your language to harness your words to work for, not against, you; select words that create a visual of the desired outcome; and choose each word as if it mattered. You might be surprised how much it does.

3. Aligning Your Actions

If a picture is worth a thousand words, than action is worth many more. Imagine five frogs sitting side by side on a waterlogged branch floating in the water. Four of the frogs decide to jump in. Now how many are on the branch?

The answer makes me smile. There are still five frogs sitting on the branch because there's a difference between deciding and doing. That difference separates performance. You may decide you want to see the elephant; you may decide you should develop Big Team thinking; you may even decide aligning your mindset with your actions is important. But until you do it, you'll remain in the company of fellow deciders, watching doers who are *winning at working*. As the saying goes, this is "where the rubber hits the road."

We can't change our past, but we can influence our future. You can't change how you've done, but you can change how you will do. Start by aligning your actions. Your future work life is about the choices you still have to make and the actions you will take. When you connect the dots and see the elephant and then take action in accordance with that big picture, you'll make better decisions, develop on-target ideas, and deliver stronger results. You'll recognize emerging opportunities, capitalize on directional changes, and discover more interesting work. Aligning your actions will change your actions, and both you and the company will benefit.

Let's look at two simple examples: John's and Mary's actions aligned with company values.

* John works for a company with a promotion-from-within culture. It stems from the company's value of personal growth and development. Yet John's actions are out of sync with that culture. He's hired from the outside for every open position in his department. He has no staff-development initiatives and refuses to allow staff to attend training since he feels it's "a waste of time." Since his department meets its overall goals and objectives, John thinks he's doing a very good job. But his first performance review tells him something different.

* Mary was used to a large client-entertainment budget in her previous public relations position. However, she quickly noticed that her new company was more fiscally and socially conservative. So she checked before her first business trip on what the usual and appropriate client expenses and entertainment avenues might include. Mary now enjoys the challenge of developing creative approaches within those company values.

Just because you've connected the dots, glimpsed the big picture (elephant), and aligned yourself with your organization's vision, values, goals, and objectives, it doesn't mean you can relax. The elephant can and does change. When it does, you must change your actions accordingly.

As Claude Bernard cautions, "It is what we think we know already that often prevents us from learning."

Dot connecting is an ongoing process. It provides insight into what actions you should be taking now, plus what skills you should to be developing, honing, and practicing for later.

Ever wonder how fish, birds, and wildebeests in huge numbers turn simultaneously? Princeton University biologist Simon Levin worked on that puzzle, and his resulting research was summarized in *Discover* magazine: "Using a computer model, Levin's team found that no communication is necessary. All that is required is for any one of a few individuals to have a strong preference for a certain direction. When one of these individuals turns, everyone turns. If no one else turns, the individual gets back in the pack as a follower." According to Levin, "It doesn't take much to direct the whole."

"Cause Something to Happen." These words hung in the locker room of football's legendary coach, Bear Bryant. I would add, if you want to be *winning at working*, cause something to happen in harmony with your company's vision, values, goals, and objectives. Action does something to more than birds and wildebeests. It causes reaction and further action in the people around us. You'll find aligned action creates an effect worth more than a thousand words.

A CHOICE . . .

Some days, I can't differentiate the small things from the not so small. Everything seems important as I struggle for understanding from collected bits and pieces. These are the days I lack perspective. I find myself overreacting to a situation, only to learn later the facts that put things in context. Or feeling afraid or resistant to something new, only to discover a great experience. Or getting righteous over my position or angry about an issue, only a month later to forget why I thought it was important. These are the days I ignore the rearview mirror warning me that objects are closer than they appear. These are the days I definitely don't see the elephant.

But then there are days when I do. On these days, perspective keeps me from digging in, thinking I'm right, over-reacting, being afraid, staying resistant or angry, feeling like a victim, or calling it quits. On these days, perspective helps me find my bearings and differentiate what really matters. Gaining perspective allows me to let go of small issues, find the important ones in my work and life, and begin to embrace a bigger world.

I want to see the whole elephant. But I have a choice on how. I can let my perspective increase gradually over time as I gain experience, or I can actively develop it. When I choose to do the latter, my career results change. Like an architect taught to design by looking at something within a narrow context first, and then viewing it from larger and larger angles, I've learned to view work and life situations from different and larger vantage points, growing "new eyes" as I go. But it requires continuous choice and focus.

You have that choice, too. You can actively develop your perspective starting right now, increasing your *winning at working* results when you do, or you can wait for your experiences to aid your sight. But there's a risk. If you make better decisions, come up with better ideas, leverage better career opportunities, and discover a bigger world by seeing the elephant, you'll never go back.

4

THE STORIES YOU TELL

"Our choices rather than our abilities show us what we truly are." **J.K. Rowling**

The way to begin a chapter on the stories we tell is to tell one.

Nestled on a pillowed couch next to a woman I barely knew, surrounded by seven other women I knew little about, I felt awkward and uncomfortable as an introverted, newbie member of an established book club, wondering if I'd made a mistake in coming to this holiday luncheon.

Having moved from corporate executive to independent writer, and from suburban Philadelphia to small town Montana, I'd accepted an invitation to join the book club from an acquaintance I'd first met when hitting (let's make that trying to hit) golf balls on a local practice range. I turned down her first invitation to join, but when she asked again the next year, I decided to give it a try. She was a gracious sponsor, taking me with her to the first few meetings, making introductions, and warmly welcoming me to the group. I'd never belonged to a book club before, and I found myself enjoying the thoughtful exchange with bright, engaging women.

But with four meetings under my belt, today felt different. Today, I didn't have a book theme to hide behind. Today, we were sharing stories. We'd been asked to bring a favorite Christmas story to read and a childhood photo to share. For several weeks, I'd agonized over the story I would read. Finally, I decided to bring two in case my favorite, a more spiritual story, seemed inappropriate. Until my foot hit the accelerator on my snowy driveway, I'd harbored the thought of not going.

It only took one volunteer to begin reading for the story-trance to envelop us. Like children, we were basking by the fire in a glorious afternoon of story time. Some stories made us laugh; some made us reach for tissues; some touched our hearts. But one particular story about quilts and the tragic loss behind the reader's story choice touched my soul.

What happened that day is the power of story. Those stories connected and inspired us. They helped us understand each other a bit better and created a greater sense of community. My choice of the spiritual story disclosed something about me to the group, and I ascertained more about them from the stories they read and told. Our story exchange that wintry afternoon confirmed for me that this was, indeed, a group where I belonged.

Just as fables and fairytales helped us learn about the world as children, life stories help us remember our humanity and establish community as adults. Stories influence us. They help us understand each other and navigate the world around us. The science behind why is described by Kay Young, PhD, and Jeffrey Saver, MD: "Narrative is the inescapable frame of human experience. While we can be trained to think in geometrical shapes, patterns of sounds, poetry, movement, syllogisms, what predominates or fundamentally constitutes our consciousness is the understanding of self and world in story."

It seems our brains are wired for stories. Young and Saver's research found that "Brain-injured individuals may lose their linguistic or visuospatial competencies and still be recognizably the same persons. Individuals who have lost the ability to construct narrative, however, have lost their selves."

Religious texts, myths, fables, fairytales, legends, and folktales all involve stories that teach, entertain, and hand down values, rules, expectations, warnings, and wisdom to future generations. Many are filled with universal themes that speak to our collective humanity, or as Carl Jung postulated, our "collective unconscious."

Stories can inspire or deceive, motivate or manipulate, challenge or deflate, persuade or console, unite or divide, ignite or resolve, anger or connect. None of this is new news. Stories are everywhere, all the time—in the papers we read, in the content we watch or listen to, and in the places we frequent.

We are all storytellers, at home and at work. And the stories we tell make a powerful difference in the results we get and the impact we have. That's what this chapter is about.

TELLING STORIES

When I was promoted to a vice president, my boss, right after congratulating me, told me a story. I recognize it now as a teaching story he deliberately shared. Instead of lecturing me on the business pitfalls of unaligned messages or the importance of speaking with one voice as part of a senior-management team, he chose to tell me a story about a boss he once worked for and the color red. It went something like this.

Challenged by a dogmatic new leader, a group of seasoned executives debated the right strategy for a new business endeavor. Each person seated at the round boardroom table had strong opinions. Each wanted to impress the new boss. None yielded his position. Some of the group advocated the yellow approach, some the blue, some the green, and some the red.

Finally after three hours, the boss said, "Red is the way we're going. That's the strategy that makes the most sense to me." Sensing the meeting was ending, the group gathered their papers and headed toward the closed door. "One more thing," he added. "Here's the way it's going to work around here. You are free to argue, debate, challenge, and even dislike each other when you're in this room. But all that stays in this room. Once the direction is decided, and you walk out that door, it's the color red."

There was no mistaking my boss's direction. And unlike much of what I've forgotten, I've never forgotten that story. I've told it to management teams I've led, and the phrase, "remember the color red," was all anyone needed to say after a heated debate.

But let's rewind and consider a few possibilities of what could have happened after that meeting. Let's say the color-yellow advocate called his staff together and said: "Well, I'm sure you're wondering what was decided. You should know, there was a lot of discussion and debate. We considered all options thoroughly and decided that the best approach was the color red. So, let's talk about what we need to do to help make that happen."

Alternately, let's say the story told by another attendee to his staff went like this: "It was a tough meeting today. And I hate to tell you, but we lost. I did my best to persuade the "new guy" that the best approach was color blue. But, he doesn't get this business yet. Mark my words, color red is doomed."

The color-yellow advocate chose to tell a story in alignment with the color-red directive. The second man didn't. He did what many of us do. He told an automatic story fueled by frustration, irritation, or disappointment. That kind of story, the shoot-from-the-hip, diarrhea-of-the-mouth venting type is damaging. Like toxins dumped into the culture, stories told without consideration can poison work relationships, build walls, and affect careers.

I've turned down candidates for hire, transfer, and promotion solely because of the stories they told about themselves (victim) and others (blaming). Their stories provided insight about who they were, how they operated, and what they valued. I agree with writer Leo Aikman: "You can tell more about a person by what he says about others than you can by what others say about him."

YOUR STORY-FACTOR

The stories we choose to tell influence how we're perceived at work: team player or not team player, victim or problem solver, resilient or discouraged, approachable or distant. They influence the culture we help to create at work: trusting or distrusting, silos or teams, soul enhancing or soul depleting. Most importantly, they affect how we see ourselves. Your choice of stories matters, increasing or decreasing your potential to be *hitting your stride.*

The most important story told at work is the one you tell about yourself, to yourself. For me, one of those is that I'm technically challenged. Okay, I know what you're probably thinking, and you're right. The more I tell myself the story of my technical incompetence, the more likely it is that my behavior lives up to my expectations. That's true on the reverse side, too. Another self-story for my life is that I can invent the future that I want to face. In both cases, as T. Harv Eker puts it, "You will live into your story."

Kyle Maynard is an example. Before he was nineteen he was a Wrestling Hall of Famer with the impressive title of the "World's Strongest Teen." He's been living into his story, summarized by the title of his book, *No Excuses.* Kyle has a congenital condition called *quadramenbral phocomelia*, with no limbs below the elbows and knees. His becoming a wrestling champion goes beyond normally impressive feats. But Kyle lives his "no excuses" story not only in the wrestling arena, but also in all parts of his life, learning to type fifty words a minute and drive a car.

We also tell stories about ourselves to co-workers. Some we edit or embellish. Like writer James Frey—who was involved in controversy over his Oprah book club selected memoir, *A Million Little Pieces*—we may fictionalize life elements. I've fired people for embellishing resumes, fabricating workplace altercations, and weaving lies. And while most of us never cross that line, there is a difference between telling our story and spinning it. Spin involves a special or favorable emphasis, interpretation, or conclusion. In some companies, managers are perceived as putting spin on messages to get buy-in from employees.

What stories are you building your life around? Are they enhancing your potential or minimizing it? Sometimes we're not even aware of the stories we've adopted as our own. We've grown up hearing about who we are, what we're like, and what abilities we have or don't have, and we overlay that story-factor onto our life. But here's the wonderful thing about stories. We can write new ones.

For much of my life, a story I lived into was being quiet and shy. It was true I was a very shy child, but I kept the story alive as I grew older. At times, it kept me on the sidelines as a spectator to my life. But now I find that story confining, limiting, and detrimental to the work I want to do. So I've let go of it and replaced it with one that better fits this stage of who I am and what I'm about. I've chosen a different story to live into. What I've learned about my story-factor is this: I hold the pen that writes my life story. If I don't like the way it's heading, I can rewrite that story.

If your story is a victim story, then you'll find problems. If it's about *winning at working* and achieving your life's potential, you'll see challenges to meet. It's not about the words, but the vision behind them. How you see your life is how you live it.

According to Annette Simmons, author of *The Story Factor*:

> People need story to organize their thoughts and make sense of things. In fact, anyone you attempt to influence already has a story. They may not be aware of the stories they are telling themselves, but they exist. Some people have stories that make them feel powerful. Others have a victim story, a story that proves your issue is not your problem, or a story that justifies their anger, frustration, anxiety, or depression. If you tell them a story that makes better sense to them you can reframe the way they organize their thoughts, the meanings they draw, and thus the actions they take.

Ultimately the stories you tell are choices you make. Whether these choices help or hurt you is within your control. Your stories have the power to influence yourself and others. How you use that influence speaks to whether you are offering the best of who you are.

One thing I've learned is you can't go wrong when you use your heart as a guide. As Oprah puts it, "The secret to being successful is to find a way to bring yourself through, even in your stories. People are looking for the essence of your truth. When you can bring your own truth to it, that's when it works."

REFLECTIVE THINKING EXERCISE: STORYTELLING SELF-AWARENESS

As you think about your storytelling choices and the power you have to influence others with the stories you decide to tell, the self-awareness questions below may provide insights for you to consider. I offer no scoring on this exercise, believing your *winning at working* approach will guide the choices.

True or False
1. When I hear a good rumor or "gotcha" story, I rarely repeat it.
2. I use storytelling to make a difficult point or to teach or inspire others.
3. I think about the impact a story will have before I tell it.
4. I rarely add spin to my stories, telling them from personal truths.
5. People would say I tell more hero than victim stories.
6. I remember stories that have influenced my life.
7. I believe I am accountable for the stories I share and repeat.
8. Stories help me understand what's valued and rewarded.
9. I positively influence the work culture through my storytelling.
10. I pay attention to the stories I tell myself, about myself.

STORY DYNAMICS AT WORK
What stories you tell, listen to, and allow to influence you

will have a powerful effect on *hitting your stride*. Learning the power of story at work, how to decipher the essential elements, and how to recognize their impact took me years to figure out. Once I did, I found these skills were instrumental in helping me to successfully navigate work environments. There are three story dynamics I found particularly useful to understand and apply at work. They include: Planting Seeds, Company Ears, and Cross-Pollination.

1. Planting Seeds

There are few things about my grandmother, other than my father, that I consider positive. At twelve, reduced to tears by her words, my mother whispered, "You don't have to love her just because she's related to you." That ah-ha moment helped me cope with a grandmother who used storytelling to manipulate and influence, to orchestrate outcomes, and plant seeds of doubt.

"Frank, I hate to be the one to tell you," the man in the grease-covered overalls paused, gathering courage to inform his partner, "your wife is causing a stir, again." A gentle man of few words, my grandfather nodded. Five months later, Grandpa Schindler moved his family from an eight-street South Dakota town to a larger one.

He knew his wife's friendly ways went over well at first, until neighbors caught on to her attaching her thoughts to other people's names. She might tell you that Hazel said, "She doesn't understand why you can't control your eating and are getting so fat." Of course, Hazel never said any such thing. Later, Grandma would tell Hazel something you said about her, which of course you never did. Success was measured by the tension she fueled between people.

My grandmother had tried this approach on my parents early in their marriage. Unlike the unsuspecting townsfolk who often didn't question what she had said, my parents, despite a few angry and painful months, did. Today, I can thank Grandma for teaching me to watch out for ill-intentioned storytellers.

There are people in the workplace who model my

grandmother's storytelling approach. They plant seeds of doubt, using storytelling to manipulate, create conflict, build walls, damage a competitor's reputation, destroy confidence, or fulfill any number of negative intentions. While these people are a tiny portion of the people we encounter, they do exist and often have an impact larger than their numbers.

Then there are the people who tell stories of possibility, hope, and triumph. They use every opportunity to plant seeds of inspiration, cooperation, and teamwork. Their stories help us embrace bigger goals and authentic selves, turning can't-do thoughts into can-do results. We remember their stories. And we remember them.

My ninth-grade social studies teacher, Mr. Jones, was one of those people. It was Mr. Jones who planted seeds of possibility in my head. In a few words, he changed what I thought I could do or even be. I don't know if he's the person who helped me become a writer; but I do know his encouraging words allowed me to harbor the thought that I could. And now, I am.

Planting seeds is a storytelling choice we make. We can plant seeds that grow work-culture "weeds" or work-culture "flowers." I'm not referring to one seed planted here or there, but a consistent approach to the stories we tell. Influence is a process that grows with time.

2. Company Ears

I don't know exactly who "they" are, but they are blamed for much of what troubles the work world. What's out on the rumor mill often reflects "their" deeds. You might have heard comments about "them" in your workplace. You may have even made some. Comments like:

"Can you believe it? Did you hear what *they* are going to do now?"

"I heard *they* decided to cut our increases so *they* could get bonuses."

"*They* promoted that idiot—what were *they* thinking?"

"*They* dumped the problem on us, and now we have to fix it."

Word of mouth has the latest complaint, infraction, aberration, or concern spreading like melted butter on pancakes. But here's the thing. More often than not, rumors and "they" stories are wrong, incomplete, or inaccurate. Passing along those rumor stories helps no one. It may seem fun in the immediate moment, but long term, it carves a large "us" versus "them" divide. One thing I learned as I advanced into higher and different management roles is how limited my perspective had been. Things are not always as they seem.

We have a responsibility to our best self and the workplace we envision not to pass on rumor-mill or "gotcha" stories intended to damage others. That behavior is more win-lose than *winning at working*. When I was more aligned with wanting to "win" versus understanding what it means to be "winning," I used to tell those "gotcha" stories, until I realized I was perpetuating what I disliked in the environment.

This is not about being a good, company citizen. It's about being a soul-filled you. When we tell or repeat vindictive, hurtful rumors or stories, we hurt ourselves by chipping away at our self-respect, integrity, and best self. We put toxins into a shared culture.

We also have an obligation to correct incorrect stories. If we have facts and accurate information, we should provide it, assuming doing so is appropriate within the company's confidential information concepts. If we can offer input or an alternate perspective, we should. For example, if someone said to me, "Can you believe they promoted that idiot, Joe?" and I had a positive story about my dealings with Joe, I'd tell it. It might be a simple story. Something like, "I don't know him that well. But I do know he's amazing in a crisis. When I was working on XYZ project, if it hadn't been for Joe's help with the system, we'd never have made the deadline."

What I'm suggesting is not the party line or offering management spin. It's offering the truth as you know it, telling more of the story, showing an alternate perspective, offering facts, and helping others see more of the elephant. That's *winning at working*.

3. Cross-Pollination

If you have an object and I have an object, we have two objects together. If we exchange these objects, we each still have only one object, and two objects between us. But if you have one idea and I have one idea, and we exchange those ideas, now you have two and I have two—and between us we have four.

Sharing ideas leads to fresh thinking and hybrid ideas that neither person might have contemplated before. That's cross-pollination in the business world, akin to the plant world, where plant pollen from one plant is used to pollinate another, producing seeds by the targeted plant, which in turn grow into a hybrid of the two original plants.

How, you may be asking, does all this relate to the stories you tell? First, cross-pollination is good for a healthy, invigorating work culture. Ideas create jobs, growth, and future opportunities. To be competitive now and into the future, the most successful companies will develop work climates where people share ideas and work outside of traditional boundaries and organizational charts to produce innovation and bottom-line results that ensure long-term success. We need work environments where we can offer the best of who we are. Helping to create those environments helps you.

Secondly, be the bee. I used to give that advice to the teams I led, and it's the counsel I give to you. Help cross-pollinate ideas, programs, and processes by sharing stories. When you happen across something wonderful in another department, mention it to the other people or departments that might have an interest. But don't stop there. Powerful cross-pollination happens when you share positive stories you've heard with the individual or department central to the story. We all like to hear those fly-on-the-wall stories about our work that we would never have known unless someone told us. And it's funny how you warm to people when you know they like your work.

NAN'S TEN STORY-THINKING ESSENTIALS

Below are my personal essentials concerning workplace stories. They've been gleaned in bits and pieces and collected mostly through my errors in judgment, naiveté, inexperience, and mistakes. I hope they help you navigate your own work journey.

1. Think Loudspeaker
   Assume that when you tell someone in confidence something about yourself or about someone you work with or for, it may make the company's informal communication network. Consider the frequency of conversations that start: "Don't tell anyone, but . . ." Then the person proceeds to tell you something they were told in confidence or were privy to in a meeting or conversation.

2. Think Reckless Driving
   Swapping bosses-are-idiots stories is common work practice and the workplace equivalent of reckless driving. If you think your boss will never find out, reread tip one. If you think it doesn't reflect on you, keep reading. Not only does this ritual keep you in the us versus them group, without even knowing it, it says something about you. Choose your stories wisely, as stories told are telling about the teller.

3. Think Intent
   "Stories are told to convey the history of the organization as told by the storyteller," according to William Rothman, professor of workforce education and development at Penn State. As Professor Rothman notes, "Watch out who the storyteller is—and what is his or her agenda." I would add: beware of your agenda. Pause and ask yourself, "Why am I telling this story?"

4. Think Yellow Light
   Things are not always as they are told. Caution is applicable in judging story truth at work, or anywhere else for that matter. I like Buddha's thoughts: "Believe nothing because a so-called wise man said it; believe nothing because a belief is generally held; believe nothing because it is

written in ancient books; believe nothing because it is said to be of divine origin; believe nothing because someone else believes it; believe only what you yourself test and judge to be true."

5. Think Choice

   "The Storyteller's Rule of Thumb," according to Peggy C. Neuhauser, author of *Corporate Legends & Lore*, is this: "Any topic or series of events can be told as a positive story or a negative story. It all depends on the telling." Her statement is applicable when listening to stories or telling your own.

6. Think Lenses

   People interpret workplace stories through differing lenses. Personal beliefs, likes, dislikes, biases, filters, as well as work, educational, and life experiences determine how we interpret the stories we hear. We translate within the context of our perspectives, adding meaning, ignoring elements, or latching onto pieces that speak to us or are philosophically aligned with our thinking (e.g., politics or religion). So don't believe that what you heard is the same story someone else did, or that the story you told is the one they heard.

7. Think Legacy

   When you've left a job or a company, the stories you've told don't leave with you. Once released into the culture, they can remain to be told again and again. If they're inspirational stories, they may continue to influence and guide those you left behind. If they're not, they may continue to leverage your original intent, good or not so good.

8. Think Power

   Stories influence. Good stories can even change behavior. Annette Simmons, in *The Story Factor*, says this: "The power to influence is often associated with force, the ability to make someone do what you want them to do. This suggests a push strategy. However, story is a pull strategy—more like a powerful magnet than a bulldozer." She explains the psychology behind that influence this way: "A story lets them decide for themselves—one of the great secrets of true influence. Other methods of influence—persuasion, bribery, or charismatic appeals—are push strategies. If your story is good enough, people—of their own free will—come to the conclusion they can trust you and the message you bring." Anything with this magnitude of power should have a warning label: User Beware.

9. Think Heart and Truth

I learned the importance of telling heart stories from a colleague years ago. He drew me aside one day to tell me how much he respected my work. But, he confessed, "I'm not sure I can trust you because I don't know your heart. You never share your stories." He was right. I rarely told personal stories at work. But his candid comments helped me change my style, realizing I was distancing myself and limiting my personal connections. Stories told from the heart weave a tapestry for trust and understanding. They contain universal truths like struggle, love, frustration, resentment, anger, pain, triumph, or loss that we all relate to. Most of us want to trust the people we work with. Heart stories help us do that by finding common truths and connections. As Virginia Woolf said, "If you do not tell the truth about yourself, you cannot tell it about other people."

10. Think Vision

What kind of workplace do you want to work in? I find that question important when deciding what stories to repeat or share. Holding a workplace vision helps me make storytelling decisions in alignment. There are plenty of stories I could tell, but they run counter to the place I want to work. I want a built-to-last culture that values differences, embraces honest and open dialogue, operates with integrity and trust, inspires soulful best-of-who-you-are behaviors, encourages big dreams, thinks long-term impact over short-term gain, has a musketeer philosophy of "one for all and all for one," understands "winning" over "win," encourages independent thinking, gives back to the world, and is run by passionate, committed people. When I hold that vision, it's easy to know which stories to tell, and easy to find the storytellers I want to work with.

REFLECTIVE THINKING EXERCISE: THE STORIES YOU TELL

Consider the following:
Personal insight is more likely if you write your answers.

1. What story, or stories, are you living into?
2. What stories do you tell yourself that positively affect your work?
3. What stories do you tell yourself that negatively affect your work? What can you do to change that?
4. What stories have you adopted from ones you were told as a child? Are they helping you at work? Do you want to keep them or let them go?
5. What life story most influences who you are? Why? Should you keep that story or begin a new one for your life?
6. Are the stories you tell at work more automatic or considered? What does that tell you?
7. Are the stories you tell more fiction or nonfiction?
8. What's the last story you remember hearing at work? Did it influence you? Why or why not?
9. What's the last story you told at work? Why did you tell it?
10. Think of a memorable work story. What makes it memorable? Have you ever retold that story? Why or why not?

You can decide which stories you tell, live into, and allow to pull you in. But that's not enough if you want to be *winning at working.* You also need to identify key puzzle pieces that offer navigational insights to your specific work culture. Those pieces are found in the stories. They're hidden beneath the orientation programs, employee handbooks, management speeches, and public relations campaigns. Woven into the fabric of your workplace is a wealth of information that can successfully aid you in *winning at working.* The challenge is to discover where they're hidden. The next section is intended to help you differentiate which work stories are important and how to find them.

NOT THE EMPLOYEE HANDBOOK

"Dissected maps" were popular in the late eighteenth century. A map was drawn on a sheet of wood, then the wood sawed into irregular pieces. These forerunners of jigsaw puzzles were used to teach geography in England. Think of workplace stories the same way. You need bits and pieces—the stories—to learn your workplace geography.

These work stories become our roadmaps. They help us determine what's valued and what's not, educate us concerning expected behaviors, and enable us to decode our work cultures. Unless you know which stories fit the puzzle map and which ones don't, it can be a landscape full of bottomless crevices, camouflaged quicksand, mismarked road signs, and inviting dead ends. But the map is clearer, the path less treacherous, and the road signs helpful when you locate the puzzle pieces.

Of course, not all work stories you hear are the jigsaw pieces needed for your roadmap. Having authored employee handbooks, designed corporate orientation and training programs, and managed culture initiatives, I know firsthand there can be a profound difference between "what actually happens" stories versus "emerging culture" or "desired behavior" stories. This statement is not cynical, but practical. You'll find both to be important in your quest for discovering what really is valued and rewarded in your organization.

Here's an example. I took my elderly mother to a local bank to help her maneuver the document-signing process needed to transfer funds from an expiring certificate of deposit. On the wall in the lobby was a wonderful statement about how that financial institution valued every customer. It was their equivalent of a customer-service vision. The reality was different. It's been a long time since I've encountered such poor attempts at customer interactions. What should have taken five minutes took fifty-five.

If you were an employee at that bank, what you heard from the "corporate story" about the importance of customer service is not a helpful map piece. The piece you need is the behavior that gets rewarded, and that's the same in every size company or business endeavor. The behavior that gets rewarded is the behavior that gets done. Those are the stories to find. At the bank, customer handoff from one associate to the next, with no one accountable, was the behavior. That made me think there was a customer-productivity measure rewarding the number of customers dealt with, not the service provided.

The key to finding a workplace roadmap is figuring out what's being rewarded. That's not as easy as it sounds. Don't confuse rewards only with something positive. Say a local pizza company decides to reward drivers for on-time delivery. Sounds good, but in actuality, they'd be rewarding speeding and reckless driving. And the "hero" stories within that workplace would reinforce speed over good judgment, even though the company value of "safety first" is written in every handbook, orientation program, and plaque.

How about the Texas school district in the news? It wanted to reward teachers for raising test scores. But it turns out the school district was rewarding numbers over methods. As a result, one school held back 75 percent of ninth graders so lower-achieving students would not participate in tenth-grade tests, and the school's staff was rewarded for achieving their goal. You can imagine the "hero" and "victim" stories told in that culture's folklore.

Notice who gets promoted, heads projects, is asked to join the teams you want to be on, or is assigned the work you're interested in doing. Then listen to the stories about those people. What do the stories tell you about the be-havior that is being rewarded in your work group? Are those "stars" playing it safe or taking risks? Are they independent thinkers or company mantra promoters? Are they there nights and weekends, answering every e-mail the same day, or off-site with clients and slower to respond? There's no right or wrong. It is what is. When you assemble those jigsaw pieces, you'll see what your work culture values and rewards. Then you can model your behavior accordingly, or not; try to change it, or not; but at least you'll better understand it.

There is a public face to workplace storytelling. Those stories are found in annual reports, orientation programs, company materials, management conferences, and training programs. But the private face is found by tapping into company folktales. These hero, villain, bootstrap stories offer insights on what really is valued and rewarded in an organization. Corporate folktales identify successful behaviors, desired characteristics, and acceptable risk taking.

When you tune in to the story network at your work, you'll discover an often untapped roadmap to aid your navigation. When you transform storytelling from an automatic reaction to a considered decision, you'll discover new ways to make a difference and offer the best of who you are to the workplace. When you unmask the story-factor in your life, you'll open new possibilities.

5

IT'S NOT ABOUT YOU

"We don't see things as they are; we see things as we are."
Anais Nin

I started my career believing that the people above me, those in positions of power and authority, were in those roles for a reason. And I was right. They were there for a reason. But the reasons weren't necessarily the ones I thought they were.

I thought people were promoted to higher and higher levels of responsibility because they were the best qualified, the most competent, the best of the best. I believed people who got ahead deserved it, based on merit or established corporate criteria. Many times, that's exactly what happens. Many times, it's not. This chapter explains why.

A few years into my working life, I started wondering how Sam was in the position he was and how Marsha, who appeared less than competent, could have the title she did. You probably know people who are in positions that make you scratch your head. How does it happen? Why did they get the job? Or maybe, why didn't you? You may think it's because of something you did or didn't do, something you need to improve or change. Yet in reality, the decision wasn't about you at all.

When I entered senior management, I started to understand. Let me be clear. This is not corporate sour grapes or finger pointing or judgmental commentary. I understand why it's not about you because I've been there. As an executive, I've made decisions on factors other than the merit or talent or performance of the person. I've made decisions on all sorts of parameters, many of them visible and many of them invisible. So have my colleagues.

You make the best business decisions you can based on who you are, what you know at the time, and the circumstances and pressures facing you. Business is business, after all. But there's a twist we often miss. Contrary to the popular myth that there's only one bottom-line—there are many bottom-lines affecting business decisions. These factors are outside of your control. I've put them in three buckets and labeled them money-line, comfort-line, and time-line, and created a fable to illustrate each.

MONEY-LINE

Once upon a time, in the place where the river runs into the sea, there lived a wise man. At least everyone said he was wise, so people believed it to be true. One ordinary day, the King and Queen sent a messenger to request that the wise man travel to the palace to solve a quandary for them. He was delighted to be of service.

When he arrived, the King and Queen explained to the wise man that they had tried for years to decide which of their triplets, two sons and a daughter, should succeed them. But each time they came close to agreeing, something happened to dissuade their views. Now, as was the law, when both the King and Queen reached five decades six, they had to announce their successor within twelve full moons, and so they asked the wise man to help them reach a decision.

The man was not terribly wise, but since everyone said he was, he too believed it and eagerly offered his advice. "This is what you must do," he told them. "Divide the kingdom in such a way as to create equal assets, equal challenges, and equal treasury. The child who delivers back to you the most gold coins after eleven moons should be named first successor, and so on and so forth."

The King and Queen did as the wise man counseled, calling together their sons Quince and Qubri, and their daughter, Qulene, to explain how the decision was to be reached. "At a minimum," the King added, "each of you must bring back five hundred gold coins." It was a sizeable challenge.

The King and Queen's children shared many traits as triplets: good looks, cleverness, responsibility, quick wit, physical strength, and determination. But they differed greatly, too, as each child had been blessed with two unique talents and one challenging trait.

Quince's challenge was the way he saw the world. He could not see grey. His world was black or white, wonderful or terrible, right or wrong, success or failure. But he was uniquely talented as a negotiator and a man of immense focus, and so he began his task.

Quince reasoned that the best way for him to build gold coins was to reduce the outflow of the treasury he had been given. So he did just that. He eliminated the Celebration of Spring Festival, reduced the number of people hired to harvest the fall crops, asked each village to wait to light lanterns until an hour after sunset instead of at sunset, put a hold on hiring new apprentices, cut incentive bonus for weavers and traders, and started the workday at sunrise instead of an hour after. He was quite pleased with his results and returned after the eleventh moon having in excess of five hundred coins for the King and Queen.

Qubri's challenge was focus. He found it hard to stick with one thing or to stay on course with just one idea. He had so many. He was intrigued by everything and anything and was fondly referred to in the kingdom as the tangent Prince. But he was uniquely gifted with creativity, always thinking up new ideas and new ventures, and was a man who made people laugh.

Qubri believed growing money was like growing crops. You must till the ground (come up with ideas), plant the seeds (choose the ideas), water and fertilize and weed (nurture the ideas), patiently wait for the crop to grow (give the ideas time), and harvest the crop (reap the rewards of the ideas). He believed—as in farming—you must spend to grow. And so, spend he did.

Qubri came up with a list of fifteen ideas, culling it down to three. He thought carefully about each one, imagining every detail. He hired a scribe to record his thoughts while he painted a verbal picture, describing the rich details in his head of how the idea should be manifested.

Knowing that he was not a man of focus, he hired three experts, each with a particular passion well suited to one of the three ideas. One expert needed special equipment to be built by the blacksmith; another required fifty people with talents in singing; and the third requested dozens of bolts of the best cloth and four seamstresses. To each expert, Qubri gave the necessary funds.

There was much excitement over the ideas. Everyone talked about them and compared their progress and watched them grow into the vision Qubri had written. He was quite pleased with his results and returned after the eleventh moon having in excess of five hundred coins for the King and Queen.

Qulene's greatest challenge was her need to please and be liked. She often found her self-esteem in mirrors reflected by others, adopting their thoughts about her as her own. But she was uniquely gifted in relationships and communication. She believed in trusting people, and in return, people trusted her. Her natural style and approach created strong bonds with everyone, and people would do most anything for her.

Qulene gathered together all the people in her land and shared openly the task at hand. She told them of the challenge she and her brothers had been given. She answered their questions candidly. And she asked for their help. The people were eager to offer assistance.

She divided them into small groups and asked them to work for two days, coming up with suggestions and ideas on how best to meet the challenge. When they returned, Qulene was happy to see each group had long lists. After all groups had listened to all groups, Qulene gave the people a surprise banquet to thank them for their efforts. The next day the people in the land came together again, and Qulene led them in discussions as they reflected on the suggestions, voted on their choices, and together came up with a plan of action.

With a definitive approach in place, Qulene asked for volunteers, and volunteer they did. They worked on special projects, reduced expenses, shared staff, increased efficiencies, and championed new ideas. Before the eleventh moon, she gathered all the people of the land together and reported back to them on what they had achieved, thanking them with two days of holiday and merriment. She was quite pleased with their results and returned after the eleventh moon having in excess of five hundred coins for the King and Queen.

During the time the triplets had been gone, the King and Queen thought about and discussed, and thought some more and discussed . . . more of the wise man's advice. So after each child reported separately to them on their earnings, explaining how it came to be that they had the earnings they did, the King and Queen called them together.

The Queen began, "There is a succession sequence we are ready to announce, based on our challenge to you." She paused to look at her husband and then continued, "But we are no longer certain that this one result—earnings in only eleven moons—is the best selection method. So we are asking for one more piece of information. We'd like each of you to return to your respective palace wings and think about the kingdom; think about the issues it faces and the future you see for it; think about your strengths and your challenges; and most of all think about your passions and if you should be, and want to be, the one to lead this kingdom and why." The Queen paused to look at each of her three children.

The King continued, "Tomorrow morning you will address your siblings with your answers to these questions. Then the three of you together will make one succession recommendation to the Queen and me. That recommendation and the information from the challenge will be used to determine who should be given the crown."

The triplets did as requested. The next morning they

learned from each other that only one of them truly wanted and had the passion to lead the kingdom. That person was the recommendation they made together to their parents. The King and the Queen thought their children very wise, and concurred.

While corporate tales rarely end as our folktale did, money-line decisions are as intricately woven. I've made difficult, sometimes personally hard-to-execute money-line decisions when I had profit and loss accountabilities. I've eliminated positions and staff, reduced budgets, denied requisitions, and frozen hiring. I've also invested profits in expansions, new positions, equipment, and ideas. Some people benefited by those decisions and others didn't. But the decisions were never about them as individuals. They were about the money-line bottom-line.

You see, profit was my first objective. No matter the organizational mission, staying in business must be the number one goal. I'm surprised how many people I've encountered don't get that essential concept. You're not going to have a job if your company or division goes under. That means money-line decisions take priority at times.

Quarterly projections and results, annual earnings, shareholder and/or stakeholder influences, traits and philosophies of company leaders, changing market factors, competition, bonus or incentive programs tied to fiscal results, departmental budgets along with the methodology for creating and tracking them, are all money-line factors influencing decisions. So are mergers, acquisitions, start-ups, and new ventures. Also, unfortunately, are the corporate-greed misdeeds we read about in newspapers, including illegal endeavors. The impact of money-line factors should never be underestimated.

Here are a few simple examples of money-line elements that could lead to decisions that affect you, one way or the other, but are not about you:

- ★ You're the leading candidate for a promotion in another department. When the hiring manager discusses her choice with human resources, she's alerted that your salary is in excess of the budgeted position's range. If she hires you, she won't be able to give you an increase until the ranges change. She selects her number two candidate, concerned she could not keep you satisfied without increases.

★ You've interviewed with the company three times, and your future boss indicates that you all but have the job and wants to check references. You feel confident you'll get an offer. It never comes. What you don't know is the future boss just got a new boss, and the position was combined with another to save payroll costs.

★ If Suzy's division doesn't meet its projected percentage increase, she won't get her year-end management bonus. She's always gotten her bonus. Suzy freezes all hiring and discretionary spending.

★ A new product launch is key for your company's profitability and growth. It's a bold initiative. All available resources are diverted to the new endeavor. Additional jobs are added, and additional funds are allocated to get the product to market. A shift in corporate direction shifts the type of people who are hired and promoted.

COMFORT-LINE

Once upon a time, in a far-off place, there lived a wise woman of great importance and influence. People traveled from way-far and close-near to talk with her and listen to her wisdom. They waited days, sometimes weeks, to get but one turn of the large, hand-blown sand-timer that allocated her time. Still, the wait was worth it, as the woman of great importance and influence would speak powerful words to put the seeker on the right path.

So it went for thousands and thousands and thousands of years.

Now this woman of great importance and influence was a woman who disliked whatever made her feel uncomfortable. When she was not perfectly comfortable with her surroundings or the people around her, she believed she could not tap into her wisdom-source and offer her thoughts to those who depended on her. So naturally, she surrounded herself with people comfortable to her. It wasn't a conscious thought, mind you. Nevertheless, she knew immediately if she felt comfortable or not with someone or something. So she chose people to work with who thought like her, resembled her, had the same background and values, ate the same food, and laughed at the same tales.

And so it went for thousands and thousands and thousands of years.

Until one day. The woman of great importance and influence looked up and saw no one waiting. There were no travelers outside seeking her wisdom, no travelers on the trails above her village walking down the mountain, no travelers talking to her helpers and arranging appointments.

She called her most trusted advisors to her. "Where are the seekers?" she asked. "What has happened to the people?" There was no answer. They did not know why people no longer sought out this woman of importance and influence.

"Go," she said to her advisors. "Go and find out."

And so they went—to each corner of this far-off land to discover why no one came to listen to this wise woman of importance and influence. Their hearts were heavy. And when they returned, their hearts were heavier.

But this woman was indeed a wise woman of importance and influence and thus listened intently to what each had to say. She did not interrupt or question or comment, only nodding occasionally to say, "Tell me more." When she heard all they had learned on their journeys, she went to the roof of her house and sat. She watched the sunset, the moon and the stars, and the sunrise. Then she gathered them together. "Go out," she said "and do not return until you have found one person who shares no traits with you. Then, bring that person to me."

They went out and searched and brought. Again she sent them out. And again. Until at last she was surrounded by people who did not think like her, did not look like her, did not speak like her, did not feel things like her. She was very uncomfortable. They pushed her thinking. They challenged her views. They questioned her motives. They awakened her. And when she became comfortable with their uncomfortable-ness, she sent them out into the faraway places to bring back someone who did not share one trait like them.

This she did for a thousand years, until the day there was a line of travelers outside her door waiting to see her, travelers on the trails above her village and travelers waiting for days, sometimes weeks, to hear the wisdom she had to offer.

Like the wise woman in my fable, we settle into our own comfort zones. Without thinking about it or noticing it, we make decisions in the workplace on the basis of our particular comfort-lines. We select people we "feel" we can trust, who have similar thoughts and values, or the same interests or hobbies—people who laugh at our jokes or watch the same TV shows or play the same sports. These people make us feel comfortable.

I believe comfort-line is one reason women are less likely to be chosen for the inner corporate circles still filled mostly with men. It's not that women are less talented or competent than men. Rather, men do not feel as comfortable with women as they do with other men, at least not yet. Women and men do talk a different language, see issues from different vantage points, and have different experiences and interests. Selection is often a comfort-line issue.

But there's an uncomfort-line factor as well. Strategically for the business, there are times we seek people who are unlike us, who push a different envelope, offer new ways to think, have different competencies, or come from different backgrounds than we do. Like the wise woman in our folktale, we become aware we need new ways and new people to improve our business results. In that case, we choose discomfort as the catalyst. Managers make comfort-line decisions, both comfort and discomfort, for exactly these reasons.

Comfort-line factors are not about you. But those decisions can affect you, positively or negatively. You may notice comfort-line issues in a variety of workplace situations. Here are a few examples:

- ★ New leadership arrives and brings a few key people with them. The new leaders feel comfortable with these people and trust them in an otherwise unwilling or hostile climate.
- ★ Someone should be fired for poor performance, and everyone knows it. But it doesn't happen. It's the devil we know who makes us more comfortable than the one we don't.
- ★ Company battle lines are drawn, and people are caught up in watching the power plays underway. Choosing players at critical times in power struggles is often a comfort-line decision.
- ★ A new initiative is launched, and the person chosen to head it will have direct access to your boss and your boss's boss, while he remains working for you. You want to be kept in the loop, and choose someone you're comfortable will do that.

There's one way to increase your comfort-line with people at work: be yourself. That's the element you control. Don't pretend to like what someone else likes, laugh at jokes not funny to you, feign interest in things you find boring, say what you think someone wants to hear, or go along with group-think you disagree with. Comfort comes with authenticity. People who are true to their character, personality, and spirit are refreshing and comfortable to be around.

TIME-LINE

Once upon a time, long, long ago, there lived in a faraway town a young man with dreams. He had aspirations to someday be the mayor of his beautiful town. His father, the town tailor, knew his son would grow up to be a tailor and did not encourage his dream.

But the young man felt it was his calling to do community work and to become mayor. So every afternoon when he finished at his father's tailor shop, he walked two miles into town. Some days he didn't make it all the way since he would stop and offer his services to the first person who needed help. Every evening, energized from meeting and working with people in the town, he would come home to dinner, do his chores, and immediately go upstairs to his sleeping area in the loft. There, late into the night, he would read the books he had borrowed from the library.

The young man earned quite a reputation with the townsfolk. Everyone said he was a special young man. Everyone liked him. Everyone counted on him. Everyone trusted him. He put his book knowledge into practical service for the community he loved. And so the years passed until the young man was no longer considered young.

Now in this town, the mayor's job was a special job. So every other leap year the town elders would spend three weeks and three days soliciting input from every man and woman on what problems the town faced and who the next mayor should be to help solve them. Once all the information was gathered, the elders went into the forest for three days and three nights to select who would lead the town for the next eight years. There was much to consider.

When the man was twenty-three and old enough to be mayor, his name was suggested to the town elders. But that year, the town had a terrible fire that destroyed seven businesses, eleven houses, and the only school in the land, which drew children from every town in every direction. Of course, everyone knew the children must go to school, so there was pressure to get it rebuilt before the leaves fell from the trees. So it was that the town elders selected for mayor the person who knew the most about building, and indeed the new school was built well before the leaves fell, and the people were happy . . . for a time.

The mayor who made the leaf deadline and led the way to the school being built did not know about things other than building. So by the time the elders met in the forest in eight more years, the non-building issues were numerous.

They didn't know where to start. Never in the town's history were there so many problems.

The young man, who was no longer such a young man, was a leading candidate. They discussed him again and again, but still thought he was too young for so much responsibility. He didn't have enough experience to handle such complex issues. So they offered the mayorship to someone who wasn't particularly strong in any one thing. But she had lived in the town longer than anyone else and had seen good years and not so good ones. She was considered the most experienced person because she had been around the longest. She was a Jill-of-all-trades who knew how to fix things. And the people were happy . . . for a time.

The mayor with the most experience fixed the things in the town in the ways they had been fixed before. But anytime someone had what they thought was a new idea, she would kindly tell them "that had been tried back in '00, and it didn't work." So it went until the elders returned to the forest, this time seeking a new mayor with new ideas. The townsfolk knew their town was behind other towns in the land. They still did things in the old ways, and they knew they needed to catch up with newer methods for their town to survive for the long term.

Of course, the young man who was getting no younger, was again a candidate. But this year, the elders decided that they had to make a bold move if their town was going to compete with other towns for goods and services. So for the first time ever, the elders decided to look beyond the townspeople for a mayor and offered the job to someone no one personally knew. However, they had heard good things about him. He was a man from a neighboring land, who had energy and enthusiasm and great ideas. And the people were happy . . . for a time.

The man's ideas enthralled the people of the town. They opened up town meetings to discuss them and debate them and evaluate them. And still the mayor had more and more ideas. So there were more and more meetings to discuss them. They spent many years discussing because the new mayor did not know much about implementing. So when the elders went again to the forest, only a handful of new ideas had been completed, and there was much unrest in the town.

So it was this year that the much-older "young" man seemed to be the best fit for the job. He would bring back the community feeling and help to finish building the right ideas for the town's future. He was the perfect choice, and the elders found it so easy to make their decision that they were back within two days to announce it.

When the much-older "young" man was offered the mayor's job, he was surprised and pleased and honored that they had selected him. But he told the elders, he was sorry he could not accept since he had already said "yes" to a mayorship in a neighboring town. Stunned, the elders returned to the forest. This time they were there for seven days. They went through every name again and again. They went through names of people not suggested by the townsfolk. Then they went through every name in the town. There was no one they particularly wanted to be mayor. But they knew they must select someone, and they did. And the townspeople were not very happy . . . not even for a while.

What happened in this mythical town happens in real-world business. You may benefit from time-line decisions or see opportunities narrowed or closed because of them. But those decisions are not about you, they're about time. Time-line decisions incorporate factors influenced by the passing of time, the pressure of time, or the importance of timing. Time plays a huge role in decision making. Here are a few examples:

- ★ "The WIN Approach," to quote Lou Holtz, Notre Dame Football coach, is "What's Important Now." And who can deliver it, *in time*. There is little consideration given to the long-term potential of individuals. Rather the search is myopically focused on the short term—who has the skills, right now, to deliver what's needed. You can recognize these *in time* decisions when a job outgrows the selected person in one or two years.
- ★ Right person for *the times*. This was as true for our

fictional town as it is for real companies. Like people, companies evolve, grow, and change. Someone may be perfect for launching ideas during a corporate start-up, but not be the right fit during control and belt-tightening. Company initiatives, emerging technologies, and market pressures all influence *the times,* and often determine why someone is hired or promoted.

★ The best there is, *at the time*—or sometimes, the best of the worst. Think poorly executed employee-of-the-month programs. During the first months, star employees are selected. But rather than continuing to reward behavior that differentiates performance, some managers go into obligation-mode, thinking it best to give everyone the recognition, (wrong!—but that's a topic for another book). They do the equivalent with selection, promoting the best person within a given group, *at the time*, rather than finding the best person.

★ *Time out.* Typically when organizational change occurs—new leadership, new initiatives, reorganization, downsizing, or budget restrictions—there's a company pause. During pauses, hiring and promotional decisions are put on hold or rethought. This also happens in departments or work groups and affects decision making once the pause is lifted.

★ *Waiting it out.* The 2005 wedding of Camilla to Prince Charles was an example. What seems impossible today can change with time. Work cultures and mores change. People viewed as unlikely candidates for leadership roles can rise in organizations by waiting it out.

★ *Time spent.* Aside from organizations with formal seniority systems, years of service can be a selection factor, especially with managers who believe someone "deserves it" because they've put in the time. Or they incorrectly equate years of service with years of experience.

★ *Saved by time.* Upheaval caused by layoffs or employee turnover can render decisions akin to the last person standing. Sometimes someone gets the promotion simply because they're there. They're the only one around who knows how to run the office, fix the equipment, or work the system.

★ *Changing times.* Business fluctuations, mergers, acquisitions, emerging markets, popular philosophies, technology, and competition all change what types of jobs a company needs and which people they hire, promote, or keep. The needs in the 2000s differ from the 1980s, which differed from the 1960s, which differed from 1940s. Not many blacksmiths these days.

BELIEVED THEN . . . KNOW NOW

I started my career with idealism. Let me give you the punch line: after twenty-five years in the business world, I am still idealistic. But now that idealism is tempered with reality, experience, and understanding.

Below are fifty snippets of what I thought as a young professional, and what I now know as a seasoned executive. I acquired bruises, scars, and disappointments learning some of them, but for the most part, they're an accumulation of years of experience and gained perspective. Sometimes I wonder, "Why didn't someone tell me this when I was younger?" It might have saved me a few potholes. I hope it saves you a few.

BELIEVED THEN	KNOW NOW
The most competent rise to the top.	Sometimes they do; sometimes they don't.
They see what I see—why aren't they doing something?	They don't see what I see—the view is different.
There is a right way.	There are many right ways.
My boss knows and understands what I do.	Not always—nor should he/she.

(*continued on p. 104*)

(*continued from p. 103*)

BELIEVED THEN	KNOW NOW
It's important for others to like me.	It's important for others to respect me.
I get trust by being trustworthy.	I get trust by giving trust.
People will remember how much I did for them yesterday.	Yes, but it's still about what I am doing today.
If I communicate it, they will understand.	Communication is not understanding.
People will teach me what I need to know to do my job.	Perhaps, but knowledge and skill development is always up to me.
It's important to prove myself.	It's important to be myself.

BELIEVED THEN	KNOW NOW
My boss knows how much work I have to do.	My boss is tracking lots of things, but that's probably not one of them.
No one will do things exactly the way I do.	True—some will do it better, so let go.
Holding on to things builds responsibility and power.	I can't embrace new opportunities when I'm holding on to old ones.
Getting results is what matters.	How I do what I do matters as much.
Work is a competition.	Yes, but the competition is with myself.
Title creates power and influence.	At times, but influence has no rank.
It's a simple problem to fix.	Things are more complex than they appear.
The person needs to fit the job.	The job needs to fit the person.
What I'm doing at work is important.	Not in the scheme of what really matters.
People motivate me.	I motivate myself.

BELIEVED THEN	KNOW NOW
My boss knows more than I do.	About some things—yes; some—no.
My boss's opinion is right.	Not necessarily, but he/she is my boss.
Failing is not an option.	Don't take myself too seriously.
It's important to win.	It's important to contribute.
I might look stupid if I ask the question.	I might look stupid if I don't.
If I don't win, I lose.	Sometimes when I do win, I lose.
The more I know, the easier it is.	The more I know, the harder it is.
It's okay to say, "I don't know."	It's more than okay—but then find out.
There are consequences in saying "No."	There are, but sometimes I need to.
I need to do it myself.	It's okay to ask people to help.

BELIEVED THEN	KNOW NOW
I need to work hard.	I need to deliver results.
If we have the same facts and information, we'll draw the same conclusions.	Nope. Beliefs, values, experiences, and filters affect conclusions.
If my work is good enough, I'll be discovered.	The best outcome is discovering me.
Things are fair and equitable in the workplace.	About as fair and equitable as they are in life.
People work for companies.	People work for people.
It's important to please my boss.	Not at the expense of myself.
What you tell me is true.	Maybe, or your perception of truth.
I'm going to try my best.	I'm going to do my best.
I define myself by what I do.	What I do is not who I am.
Someone else will speak up.	I'm that someone.

Believed Then	Know Now
What gets rewarded gets done.	Yes, but what I think I'm re-warding and what I am may be different.
What I share in confidence, stays in confidence.	Confidentiality is an endan-gered work behavior.
My boss will give me credit for my work.	Good bosses will.
If I were in your shoes, I'd do this.	I can never be in your shoes.
If you trust me, you'll tell me what's happening in the company.	It's not about trust; there's a difference between need-to-know and want-to-know.
This is the worst thing that could happen.	This, too, shall pass.
I have to do this.	I always have a choice.
It's hard to change.	Maybe, but I need to evolve.
I work for other people.	I really work for myself.
Work to pay the bills and get ahead.	Work to make a difference and be happy.

STAYING IN THE GAME

I've been affected by money-line, comfort-line, and time-line decisions. Sometimes I benefited, and sometimes I didn't. I've been through mergers, acquisitions, downsizings, organizational changes, personal career setbacks, and a myriad of new company initiatives. And the best lesson I learned from all of them? Stay a player.

Granted, my tactics for what that meant varied with the situation. Sometimes the safest play was to keep my head down and do my work exceedingly well until I understood the new landscape. Sometimes I rolled with the punches long enough to realize what was happening might be great for the company, but not a great long-term choice for me, so I moved on. Sometimes I helped others acclimate to the new direction or culture and found new opportunities emerging along the way. Sometimes the toll felt personal, like when a promotion was given to an outsider. Still, I stayed in the game.

I'm not saying I didn't yell, complain to friends, or go into a woe-is-me victim mode, licking my wounds for a time, or require space to sort out the divergent directional messages appearing to me like bombs in a corporate minefield. I'm not wired to change with the immediacy of a remote control. But I am wired to change. I know taking myself out of the game, retiring on the job, or sitting on the sidelines is not a viable option for *hitting my stride*. As Charles Darwin reminds us, "It is not the strongest of the species that survive, nor the most intelligent, but the one most responsive to change."

But there's more to *winning at working* than survival. To grow and thrive in the work world, you must find your resilient center and evolve. That may mean accepting painful not-about-you decisions, learning new skills, aligning with a new boss or company, changing direction, letting go of the way things used to be done, compromising approaches, or moving on.

Only 15 percent of S & P 500 companies listed at the end of the 1950s are still in existence fifty years later. In a *Fast Company* interview with Jim Collins, author of the best-selling book, *Built to Last: Successful Habits of Visionary Companies*, he advises companies to, "Preserve the core! And! Stimulate progress!" He claims, "To be built to last, you have to be built for change!"

His advice is as true for successful people as it is for successful companies. Even when money-line, comfort-line, and time-line decisions are not about you, they can feel like they are. Those are the times you need to preserve your core and stimulate your progress. Part two of *Hitting Your Stride*, "Another Way," offers insights on how. As you preserve your core and stimulate progress, you'll be able to deal with the changes coming your way.

Sure, change can be painful, difficult, and uncomfortable, but if you're open to what it brings, it may surprise you. It did me. My best lifetime career opportunity came *after* I was denied a promotion I coveted. It never would have happened if I hadn't stayed in the game. Someday the decision *will* be all about you, and you need to be ready.

6
IT'S ALL ABOUT YOU

"Sometimes you have to play a long time to be able to play like yourself." **Miles Davis**

*T*his is your life. No one is going to care as much as you what happens in it. No one is going to hand you your work dreams. And no one is going to create for you the life you want to live. Whether you had a difficult childhood, a less-than-stellar education, or more than your fair share of hardships or potholes along the way, or whether fortune shined on you day one with a fairytale life, or anywhere in between, it doesn't matter. You are where you are. Accept it and move on. What you do from here is ultimately *all* about you. And while parts of your life are not in your control, everything in this chapter is.

Once I understood that I could control the direction of my life and moved toward creating the vision I wanted, it became *my* life—not the one I thought my parents wanted for me or the one trying to please everyone or the one I thought I was suppose to live. I learned to bring the best of who I was to work, create my own luck, differentiate my performance, and make a difference at work. Interesting work, personal growth, and financial rewards *followed* that decision.

I will attest that dreams come true because mine have. But there's a secret. Dreams are realized through the magic of persistence, determination, passion, practice, focus, and hard work. They happen a step at a time, manifested over years, not weeks.

Yet wishing and hoping remain strategies people apply to work, despite the lack of results. They wish they could make more money. They hope they'll get promoted or offered a more interesting job. They wish someone will notice how hard they work. They hope the work environment improves, the boss comes to her senses, the problem goes away, or someone else solves it.

Their chance of *winning at working* is up there with becoming a millionaire on Vegas slots or holding the winning lottery ticket. And while it's not true the ostrich hides its head in the sand, many of us do, wondering why we never land our dreams. Olympic athletes don't get that way by wishing and hoping. Nor do great musicians, actors, chefs, architects, builders, teachers, lawyers, parents, or business people. And this book didn't get published by wishing it so.

> Words! Words! I'm so sick of words!
> I get words all day through;
> First from him, now from you! Is that all you blighters can do?
> Don't talk of stars burning above; If you're in love,
> Show me! Tell me no dreams filled with desire.
> If you're on fire, show me!

This chapter's mantra could be Eliza Doolittle singing "Show Me," in *My Fair Lady*. Talk doesn't pay the bills, provide interesting work, or personal growth. It also doesn't differentiate performance. People who take accountability, who get on with it, move a project forward, or demonstrate what they are capable of doing by doing it, have a long-term advantage. In the short run, talkers may gobble assignments or promotions, but long-term doers come out ahead. Think of your career more like a marathon than a sprint.

People who turn ideas into reality, on time with quality results, are valued at work because they're rare. Yet, it's easier than you may think to be one of those people. If you can do Thanksgiving dinner for twenty, you can learn to turn your work ideas into reality and put your dreams into your life by chunking your objectives into small actions. When my husband and I fell in love, we dreamed of living and working from the mountains of Montana by the time we were fifty. We chunked that dream into reality over twenty-five years.

You chunk things all the time without realizing it. Think Thanksgiving where tiny parallel projects come together at 4:00 p.m. in your dining room. You shop, clean, and do as much as possible ahead. You might bake pies, make salad, tear stuffing bread, cook giblets, and chop onions, celery, and basic ingredients before Thanksgiving Day. That morning, once the turkey is in the oven, you might peel the potatoes, set the table, make appetizers, and move everything along bit by bit, leaving gravy and rolls to finish when the turkey comes out of the oven, done. Voila! That's chunking.

Over the years, I've fine-tuned my chunking skills, learning to divide huge projects, ideas, and dreams into bite-size pieces. Chunking doesn't make a big project or a big dream easy. It makes the otherwise difficult, or near impossible, possible, allowing you to stop wishing and hoping.

Part of delivering results is the thinking behind it. So here's a question to consider. Is it better to do the work, knowing you will ultimately be rewarded for having done it, or should you wait until the reward is there before you do the work? Like the proverbial question of which came first, the chicken or the egg, people differ widely on the answer and run their careers accordingly.

Take Ralph. Passed over for promotion again, he wanted specifics on why I hadn't chosen him for a position. This was not a new conversation. I thought of Ralph as my chicken-and-egg dilemma. Ralph was the chicken. He believed he would make a great team leader, and when I promoted him, he would step up and show me how well he could lead. My position was that of egg. Prove to me you have leadership skills by demonstrating leadership in the job you have now, and I'll consider giving you the next position.

Here's the way I see it. One has more to lose by taking the position of the chicken and waiting for someone to anoint him or her than by being the egg and anointing oneself. If I'd waited to be a leader until someone offered me a leadership position, I might still be wishing and hoping for someone to notice me. When I wanted to be a manager, I did the work of a manager by taking on more and more responsibilities. And I got promoted. When I wanted to be a director, I did the work of a director, without questioning compensation or title. After proving myself, I got the job, the title, and the compensation. Same with being a vice president. Doing the job first, gave me the job. While it doesn't always work that way, it does increase your chances.

It's the same now that I'm out of a traditional environment. Take my dream of being a writer. Changing careers after twenty-something years in management, I could have waited to launch my "Winning at Working" column (www.winningatworking.com) until I secured a contract. But why would someone pay me to write without reading my words and knowing I can? I launched the column, built readership, then got the contract and the book. Chicken and egg again.

What works for me has been consistent. When I do the work first, the rewards follow. It's like exercising. Doing it gives me better results than thinking about it. No one likes to be called a chicken, so be the egg.

While wishing and hoping make you a dreamer, acting and doing make you someone who can turn dreams into reality. Want your work dreams to come true? Make them. That's precisely the point of this chapter. And it starts with self-awareness.

CREATING SELF-AWARENESS

While super-sizing is dying a public death at the hands of obesity awareness, ego-sizing continues to grow and thrive. Yet it can be as deadly to your career as unnecessary calories are to your health.

Too many people I've run across have American Idol

Syndrome (AIS). Like Idol contestants auditioning with little or no singing ability, these people believe they are good, often great, at what they do. They can't understand why they don't get the promotion, the outstanding review, or the highest pay increases. They view themselves as varsity team material, but they play with junior varsity skills.

Professor Mark R. Leary calls it the "better than average" effect, noting in his book, *The Curse of the Self: Self-Awareness, Egotism and the Quality of Human Life,* that most of us have a higher-than-average perception of ourselves, often blinding us to our shortcomings. One study mentioned by Professor Leary found, "86 percent of employees rate their job performance as above average."

This tendency to judge ourselves positively might seem the perfect prescription to the adage of believing yourself to success or thinking yourself rich. But it's not. Believing you're better than you are is self-deception, not self-confidence. Creating an accurate self-awareness requires self honesty and self-feedback.

When I was little, my father, like many fathers, told me I could be anything I wanted when I grew up. At the time, I was fascinated by archaeology, but impatience would have made me a poor archaeologist. Just because we *can* be something, doesn't mean we should. We all have talents and abilities, but they're not always in the areas we pursue. They should be. Finding and using your unique abilities is an inherent key to enhancing your opportunities at work and *hitting your stride.*

But assessing yourself can be a challenge. Getting As in high school biology, physics, and chemistry was easy. Yet as a college freshman, I got a D in biology first quarter. Stanford's bell curve put me near the class bottom. Accustomed to As, I rationalized a D at Stanford was an A or B at most schools. But I woke up and realized that to compete where I was—at this school—required more than my high school skills.

People who influence me most are those who give the hardest critiques. Stricken with a bruised ego for days, or on occasion for months, inevitably their feedback helps me make the right life choices to improve, change direction, or stay the course with intensity. In fact, the boss hardest on me is the one I thank the most. Good was not good enough if I was capable of better, and she was quick to point out when that was. No traditional feel-good, let-you-down-easy, sugarcoated feedback from her. When I was honest with myself, I knew she was right.

Step One: Be honest about your skills.

Consider the questions at the end of this section. Taking time to write your answers offers greater awareness and self-reflection. Unless you're honest about your skill levels, you can't do anything about or with them. That applies to under-sizing your skills as well. This should not be an exercise in humility or ego, but in accuracy.

Step Two: Based on your answers, check your direction.

Honest assessment offers a chance to become happier and more successful in the long term, giving you numerous choices. You can stay the course, find a playing field at your skill level, improve your skills to compete where you are, or change direction.

REFLECTIVE THINKING EXERCISE:
CREATING SELF-AWARENESS

Consider the following:

1. To what extent do I suffer from AIS (American Idol Syndrome)?
2. What skills am I ego-sizing?
3. What skills am I under-sizing?
4. Does my job require me to use more of my strengths or more of my weaknesses? Identify them. What does this tell me?
5. What strengths aren't I using at work? Why not?
6. What feedback have I received from a boss or co-worker that I didn't like? Is there anything I can take from it? Are they right?
7. What feedback have I received from a boss or co-worker

that I especially liked? Is there anything I can take from it? Are they right?

8. If I had an opportunity to change or enhance one thing about my skills at work, what would that be? What's stopping me?

9. Am I doing my best work at work? Why or why not?

10. Have I ever done my best work at work? If so, how was that job or environment the same, or different, from what I'm doing now? If not, where does my best work manifest itself?

Creating self-awareness begins with self honesty. It inhibits AIS and is a key to *winning at working*. But using self-awareness to have an impact on results requires ongoing self-feedback to keep you on course.

Plagued by migraines after being rear-ended on a California freeway by a hit-and-run driver, my treatment included biofeedback. After months of practice, I learned to increase blood flow reducing the migraine's trigger. Likewise, through intentional practice, I've learned to increase self-awareness and *winning at working* behaviors by applying regular self-feedback. Here are four of my favorites: The Whine Factor, Drainers and Boosters, Touchstones, and Pond Size.

1. The Whine Factor

Brian's work was exceptional. Yet, as his boss, I rarely offered him additional responsibilities and never thought of promoting him or selecting him for a critical project. Why? His whine factor got in his way.

Brian was quick to complain to anyone who'd listen how much work was on his plate, or how hard, or how late he worked. His whine factor was a protective shield that ensured he didn't get more work. But it also shielded him from getting the opportunity-filled assignments, more interesting work, and the highest pay raises.

Stephanie was a different story. She was masterful at weaving vivid details with a precision that explained exactly why the promised outcome didn't happen. This week it centered on a miscommunication, last week it was the delayed delivery, or the reduced advertising, an incompetent supplier, or a staff illness. Every story was accurate, every reason plausible, every explanation justifiable, always a good reason why she couldn't deliver the promised quality, precision, or timeliness. As her boss, it took me a while to understand. It took me longer to apply that understanding to my life.

Here's my take on that understanding: reduced accountability reduces results. I realized Stephanie's accountability decreased as her whine factor increased. When she became entrenched in offering reasons why something didn't happen, she became less involved in personally influencing the results.

I've seen the whine factor derail projects and people. Whining shifts a mindset from can do to can't do, allows potholes to become sink holes, turns challenges into complaints, and reframes opportunities into "woe-is-me."

Monitoring my whine factor has become second nature. When I notice it's high, I'm alerted that my actions are less accountable. It's a signal to tune in to what I personally can do to control, adjust, enhance, or correct the current course so expected results are delivered. That point is worth repeating because it differentiates performance. If you want to control the outcome, you have to get your hands calloused along the way.

Learning to listen to your own whine factor is a mechanism guiding you toward greater accountability and *winning at working* behaviors. Less whine means more accountability. Higher accountability typically means better results.

2. Drainers and Boosters

Like a balloon with air pouring out, deflated, and flat at the end, I hung up the phone, drained. For the most part, I had offered a supportive ear with occasional contributions of asked-for advice. Several days in a row, he called or stopped by my office with a second, third, and fourth verse of the same song. After each encounter—an energy zap! It got to the point where Ron's mere presence caused my energy to disappear, replaced with an empty dullness, a dumpling like heaviness, as if his negative energy was seeping into me.

Ron was an energy drainer. Some people are. If I spend much time around people with negative energy, my optimism and enthusiasm for work or life are adversely affected.

Like huge anchors on cruise ships, other people can hold you down—not intentionally, but their negativity has an effect. It's hard to be *winning at working* when you're anchored in place. It's hard to see the next great idea and enthusiastically embrace it when you're feeling a sticky heaviness. And it's hard to think creatively when you're feeling empty.

You may know people in your life who hold you down, who zap your enthusiasm, who cheer you into self-destruction, and occupy so much of your time and energy that you can't offer the best you to anyone, including yourself. And you know people who do the opposite.

My advice? Use that feedback. Spend less time with the drainers and more time with people who offer an energy boost. Once you've identified how it feels to be around energy boosters, look to fill gaps especially on work teams, with people who bring positive energy to a meeting, who are fun to be around, whose enthusiasm lifts your spirits, enhances your creativity, and adds to your work life. Find and stay close to energy boosters. Be one yourself.

I use a simple measurement to identify energy drainers and energy boosters: the laugh factor. The more laughter I find in the process of doing business, the more energy is in the room. The more energy in the room, the more gets done. I look for people with whom I can laugh, have fun, and share ideas. My work results are better when I'm around people who energize me.

3. Touchstones

A smooth, glacier-green Montana river rock sat at the corner of my desk for fourteen years, adding to a small collection of mementos I kept at work—the carved branch from my son, a pinecone from my husband, a penny from my father. To anyone else it was a pretty rock. To me, it was a tangible reminder of a dream I was working to achieve. On a particularly bad day, the kind where you fantasize walking into your boss's office and calling it quits, I would hold the smooth stone in my hand. By rubbing its surface, I was reminded of what was important and what wasn't.

I need touchstones in my life. I need ways to keep my balance, to determine if what I'm feeling or struggling with is important or genuine. Some touchstones are people I trust to offer me perspective, tell me the truth as they see it, pull me back from the edge, or push me out of a recurring cycle. Some touchstones come from the spiritual side of my life, including meditation and being in nature. Others are fluid touchstones popping in as data points along the way—reactions to my writing, a 360-feedback experience, a motivational speaker, or a candid conversation with an adversary.

To me, self-feedback without touchstones is like going to work as the emperor in the children's fable, looking only for confirmation of what you believe to be true.

4. Pond Size

I like to remember what size pond I'm in. Most of my career, I've been a medium-size fish in a medium-size pond— ponds with ten to thirty thousand people. I've done well in my pond. But I'm cognizant that a pond is not a lake or an ocean. I don't know if I'm a world-class player. I do know I'm a strong medium-size pond player. Can I play at the lake level? Maybe. I don't know for sure, but I do know the ocean is not my skill set.

It's like this. Let's say you were the best gymnast in your high school, state, and college. Were you the best in the United States? Did you win the Olympic gold? Probably not. So, on a bigger playing field of all gymnasts in the world, you might find yourself closer to the bell-curve middle. That's skill-level perspective.

If you buy shoes that fit, you don't notice your feet when

you walk. Your feet are comfortable and take you where you want to go. But if your feet hurt, every step is painful. Finding the right-size work pond is like that. Find the one that fits you, and you won't even notice. Be in a pond that doesn't, and like those ill-fitting shoes, it will give you blisters. The size of a pond doesn't matter as long as it's the right fit for you.

CORE PHILOSOPHIES

Understand a person's philosophies and you tap the core of who they are. I challenge you to reflect on yours.

You can learn more about me by knowing my values, my heart, my passions, and my dreams, then by knowing the work labels of employee, manager, mentor, catalyst, leader, or writer that I've pasted on my forehead over the years. Labels are job titles. They tell about the role, not about the person. Like my personal definition of *winning at working*, my operating philosophies have crystallized over time as well. Two central tenants have emerged: how you do what you do matters; and, you get what you give.

How You Do *What* You Do Matters

There are people on organizational rungs who use bullying techniques, intimidation approaches, obnoxious antics, and a laundry list of untrustworthy intentions. They are successful, smart, well-paid individuals who many believe they should emulate to get ahead. How they do what they do does not appear to affect their results. But it does.

By contrast, there are people on organizational rungs who offer the best of who they are at work, bringing a presence that encourages others to do the same. These people are also successful, smart, well-paid individuals, but the loyalty, enthusiasm, and discretionary efforts they evoke in others create results beyond expectation and make a difference in the work lives of those around them.

The explanation is simple. Companies can buy a presence on the job but cannot pull ideas from heads or order passions at work. These are earned by the powerfully intangible *how*. If you have doubts, consider your performance under both types of people. Both represent the how. Long term, the how always affects the what.

Yet for people interested in *winning at working,* this core philosophy is about more than the impact on results. It's about the impact on self. How you do what you do is a reflection. It's an indicator whether you're offering the best of who you are to the workplace. That best taps your core, sometimes referred to as your authentic self, and is *all* about you.

Your how will differ from mine based on personality, values, beliefs, experiences, and a host of things. With no set recipe or formula to follow, your goal should be to operate from your authentic center with integrity and well-meaning intentions. I admit, some days are easier than others. But I can feel a difference on those days when I'm *hitting my stride.* The grind is gone, replaced with a sense of fluid aliveness, a sense of "ease and grace." A life goal of mine is to operate from my authentic self all the time. It's a long journey.

Don't interpret the how to mean you should be nice at work. It's not about being nice, not getting angry, or not having conflicts. It's not a sometimes approach when business is good and things are going well. It's about being authentic, genuine, and real. Authentic people are not saint-like but self-like. The how comprises everything you do or don't do. As motivational speaker Brian Tracy puts it, "Everything counts! Everything you do helps or hurts, adds up or takes away."

My knee surgeries are an example. The first surgeon failed to fix the problem. A second surgeon did. Yet when a fall on ice tore my other meniscus, I didn't go to the orthopedist who successfully fixed the first knee. Why? He wasn't offering the best he could to me. He didn't have time for my questions, kept patients waiting excessively, lacked front-office organization, and called me "Ann." I found a surgeon who operated with both the what and the how. He corrected the problem, called me the morning after surgery, treated me as more than a knee, and had impeccable office standards and an engaging staff that built confidence. It's no surprise he's among the most respected doctors in the area.

If you don't or can't deliver the what, the how is not going to compensate for poor results. As a perfectionist, highly organized, responsive, enthusiastic, and likeable team player, Judy was still fired because she couldn't do what I hired her to do.

Assuming you deliver what your job requires, the how comes importantly into play. *How* you do *what* you do creates an impression. Like an integrated fabric, the how is your weaver's signature. That weaving can be a magnificent tapestry or a rough rope mat. Tapestries are more valued.

Your weaver's signature remains in the work and influences those around you, especially when your weaving is true to your spirit and character. Offering the best of who you are means operating from your authentic core. If you do that, the how will take care of itself.

You Get What You Give

The law of reciprocity is a core philosophy for *winning at working*, and I believe, for life. You get what you give is not a strategy. Some contend it's a law of the universe. Others chalk it up to New Age thinking. It doesn't matter what you call it as long as you understand its power in your life.

Today, I experience the law of reciprocity differently from my original expectation when I learned about it. Then, I expected a one-to-one result. I thought if I went out of my way, put extraordinary effort into a task, and produced exceptionally well, I would get back a compensated equivalent in a reasonable period of time—perhaps a raise, a promotion, or more responsibility. But I've learned it's not a trade. It's more like a boomerang that goes into the world, eventually falling where someone finds it and tosses it back. When that will happen is unknown. But it will come back.

Now I understand if I am honorable and helpful to you, of course with helpful and honorable intentions, or offer extraordinary efforts to you, at some point in my life that honor and helpfulness and extraordinary effort will be returned, maybe from you but most likely from someone else in a different way or situation.

Sometimes I notice the law of reciprocity in action when something "falls out of the sky," and I am the recipient of kindness from a stranger or trip over an apparent coincidence. Of course, the less positive side is there, too. So when I act selfishly, rudely, or angrily, I shouldn't be surprised when that shows up later in my life from someone.

The law of reciprocity is why winning at working *works.* If you offer the best you at work, you will ultimately get the best for you in return. It may not be next year or in ten years, but your best, or not best, will come back to you.

Still, it's not as easy as it sounds. Let me explain by way of an anecdote. Slowly moving my chair to the assigned group of strangers gathering to complete the conference leader's direction, my mind flashed, "I hate these things," as I introduced myself. Settling into my chair at the group's edge, I waited for a self-selected leader to emerge. Relief came as the required group presentation finished, and my anonymous comfort was restored, allowing me once again, to listen to the headlined speaker.

Replaying the weekend's highlights on the drive home, my only disappointment was the hour spent in the group exercise that yielded nothing for me. Randomly assigned to work with less-experienced individuals must have been the reason, I thought, reflecting on my limited participation.

Like a thistle lodged in my sock after a walk in the woods, my feeling of disappointment clung weeks after the conference. "Odd," I acknowledged, as the experience periodically popped to mind. Eventually, filing the feeling into a mental cabinet marked, "strange reactions," months later the proverbial ah-ha finally emerged.

I realized the lingering disappointment was disappointment in me. Viewing the exercise from what I could get from it, I missed what I could give to it. I hadn't seen it as an opportunity for giving. Deciding the group was unlikely to provide me insights, I disengaged, sitting out rather than considering my input potentially helpful to others. That ah-ha challenged my thinking about more than an hour's exercise.

I discovered I've been, at best, a sometimes practitioner of my beliefs and messages as an advocate of the law of reciprocity. Waiting for someone to give something to me before I give something to them is getting it backwards. Not doing so was my loss. I've learned I don't get trust by being trustworthy, love by being loveable, or a purposeful life by holding on to it. I get trust by trusting, love by loving, and a meaningful life by giving parts of it away.

REFLECTIVE THINKING EXERCISE: CORE PHILOSOPHIES

Consider the following:
Personal insight is more likely if you write your answers.

1. What do I uniquely have to offer others?
2. How can I better use my skills or talents in my work?
3. Think of a specific experience at work where your actions were without personal interest and for the good of the whole? How did that feel?
4. When I take center stage, what am I hoping to get? What am I giving?
5. When I sit on the sidelines, what am I hoping to get? What am I giving?
6. When does the concept, "What's in it for me?" affect my behavior?
7. I admire people who . . .?
8. I am frustrated by people who . . .?
9. What behaviors do I have in common with the people I admire and the people who frustrate me?
10. How might the law of reciprocity affect my thinking and approach at work?

FUELING YOUR PASSION

Growth for a lobster is risky business—they must hide shell-less from predators for nearly two months until a new shell is formed. Yet the lobster knows instinctively it must endure this process again and again to live.

Growth happens in many ways. Mine is frequently packaged as one of those life lessons. Some lessons reduce me to an emotional infant as vulnerable and frightened as that shell-less lobster. Some come with new characters and a new plot, yet with themes recurring so many times it's clear I still haven't gotten it. And some leave me feeling akin to Samuel Butler's view that "Life is like playing a violin solo in public and learning the instrument as one goes on." Often these strip-off-the-outer-layer lessons push me into growing. I wonder if growth is as painful for the lobster as it is for me.

Growth can come from what my husband calls, "life happens." Unexpected. Unwanted. Circumstances beyond our control that change our life. Tragedy, natural disasters, death, accidents, illness, divorce, job loss, awful bosses, mergers, relocating, and financial hardship are but a few of these "life happens" events. There's nothing we can do to change what was unwelcomingly thrust into our lives. Eventually, we may decide to move past the event, growing as we do. Or we may remain stuck in anger and pain. I've had a few of both.

Of course, not all growth is thrust upon us. There is the kind we choose. If personal growing is good, why not seek it? Working in whatever individual ways work for you, hearing the messages that seem to speak to you, you can grow, develop, change, and evolve because you want to. But choosing to grow doesn't mean it's easy. It is still difficult to shed a shell, take off a mask, or leave a comfort zone, and can still be frightening and painful when you do.

I can't say I always like this process of growing, nor the painful emotions and vulnerability I feel in its wake. But I am amazed at the capacity I have to change and grow in life, especially when I decide it's time to move past the past. I believe growing keeps me alive, in the deepest sense of the word. I am thankful I have grown and thankful I continue to grow, whether pushed or by choice. Who I am is a reflection of the growing I've done. I like that I am stronger, a bit wiser, and more loving and tolerant as a result. I have much more growing to do in my life and know some will be painful. But like the lobster, I instinctively know I must keep doing it.

So what does any of this have to do with fueling your passion?

Everything.

What I felt passionate about at twenty-five was different from thirty-five, and that was different from forty-five, and I know it is going to be different when I'm sixty-five. But if you were to ask someone to describe me at any age, "passionate" would be a word you'd hear. Yes, I'm a subscriber to the career advice that you should find and use your passion at work. Or, as I say to my son and daughter-in-law, do what you love to do and it'll work out.

But here's the kicker. Life *does* happen, and when it does, we can get pushed to the ground, passion-less. I felt that way when I got fired, and again when I lost a key promotion, and several times in between, feeling more defeated than passionate. The inscription around the foot of a sixteenth-century Scottish drinking bowl captures it: "Money lost little lost, honour lost much lost, heart lost all lost."

Fueling your passion is a key to *hitting your stride* and making your work, work for you. People with passion make things happen, delivering intangibles that manifest a competitive edge. Sometimes refueling is as simple as attending a motivational seminar, taking a class, getting involved in a new idea, or reading a book. Sometimes self-nurturing is needed, anything from a vacation to a half hour a day me-time. And sometimes it takes lobsteresque shell-shedding pain and growth.

Fueling new passions and relighting smoldering ones will keep you *winning at working*. But you must actively refuel along the way. Here are a few simple refueling ideas to add to your own:

- ★ Mentor an intern or new employee
- ★ Work a charity or organizational event you care about
- ★ Volunteer to head a new project, or work on a new team

★ Learn a new skill; take lessons in something you've always wanted to do

★ Organize your work space, clean files—get a fresh organizational start

★ Read motivational newsletters or e-zines (e.g., www.winningatworking.com)

★ Listen to motivational books-on-tape while commuting or exercising

★ Attend a seminar every six months, even if you pay

★ Write down or review life goals—complete one small action step on each

★ Write your accomplishments since last year on this date

★ Buy or borrow a motivational quote book; spend ten minutes a day reading it, or get a new quote sent to you every day (e.g., www.dailyworkvita min.com)

HOW'S YOUR DIRECTION?

Since *winning at working* is all about you, how are you doing?

Below are twenty positively viewed work behaviors, presented in no particular order, nor inclusive of all important behaviors. Rate yourself honestly on each.

REFLECTIVE ASSESSMENT EXERCISE: HOW'S YOUR DIRECTION?

On a scale of 1 to 5, rate yourself.

1 = Never 2 = Rarely 3 = Sometimes
4 = Usually 5 = Almost Always

1. Continuous improvement is a component of my approach. I work to improve the quality and efficiencies of what I do, as well as my skills.
2. I am aligned with company vision, values, goals, and

    direction, adjusting priorities and making course corrections, as needed.

3. I understand the business I work in as well as the competition, challenges, and emerging trends of the company and industry.

4. I have a strong attention to detail and a passion for personal excellence. My performance ratings confirm that.

5. I not only think about what I do, but also how I do it, recognizing that components of both affect my results.

6. No matter the level of my position, I make the best decisions I can for the long-term benefit of the company.

7. Reading trade or business publications is something I do.

8. If my job is not to work directly with the client or customer, my job orientation is to help and support those who do. I view co-workers as clients or customers.

9. I deliver what I commit to, on time and with quality, requiring limited follow-up from my boss.

10. I look for and find solutions.

11. It is important to keep people I work with and for up-to-date and informed. If anything, I over communicate.

12. I like what I do and my enthusiasm shows.

13. I answer my e-mails and voice mails within forty-eight hours.

14. I can't imagine being bored at work with the ideas I have and things I would like to improve or implement.

15. I like the people I work with. We have fun working together and delivering results.

16. My ideas are well-thought-out and tend to be accepted when presented.

17. If I can't figure things out on my own, I find people who can help me.

18. Confidential information stays confidential with me.

19. I am an "influence" leader. People seek me out and listen to my ideas and input.

20. I see myself as responsible for creating my future at work.

Self-Assessment Scoring

If your total score is above 80, feel confident you are heading

(*continued on p. 128*)

(*continued from p. 127*)
in a *winning at working* direction. If your total score is below 80, use the information for self-feedback and coaching. One suggested approach is to define a personal growth and development plan called, "Project Me." Use the chunking approach to develop an action plan for increasing your performance, achieving your goals, and positively influencing your results.

GUIDING VISION

Once I realized that *winning at working* was all about me, and I had accountability for my life, one vision served as a guiding principle at work and at home: *You invent the future that you want to face.* These words, plucked from "Future Games," a song recorded by Fleetwood Mac, are engraved in my wedding band and painted on a lintel over the kitchen sink in a Montana cabin that took twenty-five years to realize. The words continue to serve me well.

PART TWO

ANOTHER WAY

"You cannot change the music of your soul."
Katharine Hepburn

7

BRINGING YOURSELF TO WORK

"Pay attention to the nurturing of your heart— your greatest experience of success will come as a byproduct of the growth of your spirit." **Carol Orsborn**

She was no more than four, seated at the table next to ours, the only child in what appeared to be an extended family reunion at DisneyWorld. Excited exchanges and long-missed hugs erupted as adults joined the table, pausing to comment on "how big she'd gotten." After each hug, she returned to her crayons, quietly coloring Mickey, Minnie, Donald, and Goofy, until addressed directly. "So Allison, tell me, what do you want to be when you grow up?" he asked. The table quieted as eyes turned to Allison. "I want to be *me*, Granpa." she matter-of-factly stated, returning to her coloring.

If only I had been as wise as Allison. Somewhere along the way, I got my identity mixed up with my occupation. I equated who I was with what I did, linking my value as a human being with my value as an employee. With each raise or promotion or new accomplishment, I felt more valuable and important. Likewise, if my expectations of what should be were not met, my self-worth fell, falling most when I was passed over for a top job I'd built a career around achieving.

Lunching with a friend who was attempting to regain a sense of self-worth after losing his job in an economic downturn, I told him, "You're not your job. Your job is what you do, not who you are." Struggling with my own sense of failure, the words were as much for me as for him.

Now years later, with the insight of hindsight, I'm grateful I didn't get that coveted job. It was one more notch on a success driven "win" path; one more confirmation of competitiveness; one more ego boost of a bigger job title, salary, and perks; one more evolutionary step on the path I'd started fourteen years previously. Not until denied a corner office did I question my path taken, the tolls paid, and the self smothered. Not getting that job changed my life and my career, throwing me into a dimension of reflective exploration, new opportunities, enhanced personal growth, and found courage.

Now I'm clear that who I am and my worth as a human being have nothing to do with my title or paycheck or job. It took half a career for me to realize that making a living and making a life are not the same thing. I agree with Allison that when I grow up, I just want to be me. It's a lifetime process, I think, becoming who you are capable of becoming. Yet it is the most important work you can do. In fact, it *is* your work.

I liken Allison's sense of "being me" with the "it factor." *American Idol* judge Simon Cowell periodically remarks about the "it factor" when assessing contestants. It appears as nebulous, undefined, and subjective attributes one either has or doesn't have. It falls into the category of "you know it when you see it." He's right. You do know it when you see it, and that's true in the workplace, too.

Some people call it passion. And while that's part of it, it goes beyond the intense driving focus associated with passion. When I think of the hundreds of people I've hired in my career, there was one spark that yielded an unwavering "yes" decision, one spark that made me stop interviewing and put together a compelling offer, one spark worth searching unrelentingly to find.

That spark? Desire. Not a person's desire for the job, although interest and enthusiasm are always a plus. But their intention or aim—their desire for greatness. I use that word carefully. I don't mean greatness in the context of being a great or famous or distinguished person, or climbing a hierarchy to achieve status, power, or influence.

Rather, the desire for greatness I'm referring to is tied to the seeds of possibility sprouting from their talents and abilities. You see, these people with the "it factor" desire to live their life's potential. They aren't out to win. They're out to become the unique person they are, to the fullest extent of their gifts. It's that desire that fuels their drive, motivation, and persistence. It's that desire that keeps them learning and growing and stretching. It's that desire that makes them exceptional.

But most of us don't desire our own greatness. We cheat ourselves from becoming ourselves. We squander our unique gifts by copying other people's approaches and styles. We mimic others' successes thinking if we follow their path or do what they do, we'll end up at the same destination. But emulating others doesn't unleash our individual uniqueness or bring our voice to the world.

People with the "it factor" know the only path to their greatness is one of their own making. That's why you know them when you see them. These are people who stand out like a tulip in a rose garden. Russian-born choreographer George Balanchine defined them well when he said, "I don't want people who want to dance. I want people who have to dance."

But here's the thing. The "it factor" is not a limited-edition attribute. The desire to live our own greatness is available to each of us if we tap into it. It's a personal choice we can make. That's what this chapter is about—finding your "it factor" and bringing it to your work.

FINDING AND OFFERING YOUR GIFTS

What do you uniquely have to offer? What are the gifts you have to give to the world or in this case, the workplace? The answer may have everything to do with what you are doing now or nothing to do with it, or something in between.

When I wasn't selected for that coveted department-head job as expected, it wasn't the devastation and sense of failure that gnawed at my soul, it was the regret. When I moved from hurt and anger and woe-is-me-victim thinking, I regretted not being myself at work. Looking to please, impress, be liked, or win accolades, like silly putty, I morphed to be what I thought was wanted or expected, and in the process, I lost touch with my "it factor," my gifts, my light.

Yet at the time, I never thought I wasn't being me. Perhaps, if I'd paused to consider the nagging feeling that something was missing in my life, or if I'd noted my robotic busyness, punctuated by stress, frustration, and angst, or picked up on the clue that resistance and grind were leaving me as healthy as a salmon after swimming upstream. But I never consciously thought about it. I was too busy living my life from the outside in, not the inside out, until I wasn't selected and spent months in reflective self-analysis.

I decided to refocus my energy on what I could give at work, not get. That shifted my intention and even though I didn't know it at the time, my philosophy shifted from win to winning. The grinding slowed and my work began to flow as a sense of purpose emerged. When I consciously started to be me at work, to show up, and to try to make a difference in whatever ways fit my talents, work took on a new dimension. I'm convinced that's why an amazing opportunity was attracted into my life. Asked by a new company president to report directly to him, start-up a corporate department, and do work I was passionate about was almost too good to be true. But it happened, and for nearly a decade my work life was filled with personal growth and opportunity.

I found my gifts by bringing myself to work, or at least moving directionally that way, as I accepted a role outside of my then-career path and chosen field. By letting go of who I thought I was supposed to be, I stumbled on the reality of author and spiritual activist Marianne Williamson's words, "When we become who we are, we will know what we are suppose to do." That's when my career and my life took off.

I'd gotten it backwards. Lots of people do. We think we should discover our purpose in order to find ourselves, as if we're lost. But we're not lost, we're under the din of the workplace, the noise of life's challenges, the suction of fitting in, being liked, or fulfilling expectations of others. Your work is not to find your purpose, it's to become yourself. Then, your purpose finds you.

How do you do that? How do you become who you are capable of becoming? How do hear your voice amongst all the others? How do you bring yourself to work? How do you contribute your uniqueness to the world? How do you find your gifts? Here are a few ways to start:

1. Focus Your Commitment

Commitments. Commitments. Commitments. They fill our days, our heads, and our lives. Most of us are in the commitment business. Of course, that's not what we call it. At work, we're making commitments to customers, suppliers, bosses, co-workers, and staff. At home, we're making commitments to family, friends, neighbors, community, and organizations. Not to mention commitments to pay taxes, credit card bills, mortgages, and car loans.

Commitments become our drivers. Like the proverbial hamster wheel, we can't stop the stress or the time demands we obligate ourselves to because of commitments. We work so we can meet our professional, personal, and financial ones. We work so we can do the other things in our lives we want to do. We work to get the good review, the promotion, the raise, or the new job so we can get the house or the car or big vacation.

As tapestries of commitments seemingly smother us, we may feel we "have" to do something, when in fact we have a choice, though we must recognize it may be one with consequences. We may think we can't let someone else down, when in fact we can say "no." We may even believe we work for other people, when in fact we work for ourselves.

The possibility of saying "no" is viewed as a non-option for some believing they must follow their family's wishes, adhere to their upbringing, or please their boss. But when you choose to live your life, to be who you are capable of becoming, and to follow your dreams, saying "no" is a conscious choice to be *for* you, not *against* them.

When we "get" that we work for ourselves, we become the drivers, not the passengers, of our commitments. Only then does our commitment orientation change. We discover it's easier to say "no" and more gratifying to have choices. With all the commitments you make, most of us miss the most important one there is . . . the one we make to ourselves.

However, people who are *winning at working* make that commitment. Not in a selfish egocentric way, but as the author of their own life. They commit to use their unique gifts and offer the best of who they are to the world. They commit to their dreams. They commit to becoming who they are capable of becoming. Often their work is a path to do just that.

I find clear differences in people who make the commitment to self-actualization and people who don't. Self-committed people are building their skills, working on personal growth, acting like owners, and offering their talents without being asked. While others watch from the sidelines, these people are solving problems, resolving conflicts, and assisting others. They give. They take action. They make things happen. They are energized, enthusiastic, and passionate about their work. Their hearts are in it.

When you understand you're working for yourself, that's what happens. Making a self-commitment to become your best you, doesn't reduce your commitments or your work, but it does alter them. When you commit to bringing yourself to your work, in the deepest sense of that concept, something happens. That something fuels your passion and ignites your spirit. If you want to be *winning at working* and *hitting your stride*, make the most important commitment you can make. That commitment is all about you.

2. Focus Your Self-Knowledge

Early in my career, my boss told me my communication skills needed improvement. Five months later, a new boss heralded the same skill set as a significant strength. While one might conclude I'd focused on developing skills in a weak area, that wasn't the case. The difference was their opinion. It turns out, I built my career using communication strengths I knew by then I possessed.

Unfortunately, for many, noted weaknesses carry a greater feeling of workplace significance than acknowledged accomplishments or strengths. But people who are *winning at working* know that's backwards. They understand finding and maximizing strengths is their success key.

While minimizing weaknesses can be important, lasting success is achieved by maximizing strengths. People who are *winning at working* practice, learn, and stretch themselves, working to hone their talents into exceptional performance. They focus on developing their abilities to higher levels of expertise because that's where career payoff happens.

When you enhance what you do well naturally, you shine. When you find and maximize your gifts, you carve your unique success key. And when you build your self-knowledge, you lay a foundation to guide you through the winds of opinion.

That doesn't mean you shouldn't work on needed areas of growth, or develop other skill sets. That's important too, but in perspective. An Olympic hopeful sprinter can best achieve her goals by magnifying her running ability, not developing her archery prowess. Some weaknesses are unimportant. Improving others might elevate your strengths. As the German proverb reminds us, "One must carve one's life out of the wood one has."

I've watched people make strategic mistakes in their careers by focusing on weaknesses, instead of building on strengths. They spent too much time on what they didn't do well and too little polishing and enhancing what they did well. They allowed someone else's opinion, rather than their self-knowledge, to dictate direction.

3. Focus Your Future

When faced with catching a fly ball, Lucy missed again. "The past got in my eyes," she told Charlie Brown, "I thought

I had it, but suddenly I remembered all the others I'd missed."

In two decades in management, I've known hundreds of workplace Lucys. People who let their past get in the way of their future; who self-determine what they're going to do, can do, or might be able to do by what they didn't do, haven't done, or even failed at. They stay aligned to their past like a *Peanuts* comic-strip philosophy.

Past-focused people sabotage themselves with yesterday's mantras that become today's expectations:

"Yeah, we tried that before and it didn't work."

"I got rejected once already so I'm not going to make that mistake again."

"No one listens to my ideas."

What they miss is this—that may have been true yesterday, but they're in charge of deciding if it's still going to be true for them tomorrow. While people can't change their past, life is about the choices we still get to make. It's only too late when we give up, stop trying, or believe our negative self-talk press releases.

People who are *winning at working* know what happens tomorrow is affected not by yesterday, but by today. They follow a philosophy akin to my refrigerator magnet's counsel, believing "Mistakes are part of the dues one pays for a full life." They don't dwell on their mistakes, less than optimal performance, or occasional missed balls. They accept them, learn from them, and move on. Then they do something so it doesn't happen again. People who are *winning at working* are focused on what is to come.

If you want to hit your stride, don't allow yourself to be hijacked by what promotion you didn't get, the increase you're disappointed in, what potholes slowed you down, which boss didn't like you, or what opportunities you missed out on. Let the past be the past. Focus instead on what you can do now to affect your future and develop your talents and what you can do now to bring yourself to work. Don't listen to Lucy. Be about your future, not your past.

4. Focus Your Yardstick

The headline caught my eye, "The Goal: Wealth and Fame."

The article in *USA Today* examined a survey of top life goals for the college-age crowd. It surprised me that there was a 33 percent jump today, versus thirty-eight years ago, in beliefs of college freshmen that being financially well-off was "essential" or "very important." But what surprised me even more was their desire to be famous.

Perhaps it's indicative that this celebrity-obsessed culture produced freshmen defining life goals in terms of money and notoriety, putting the value of "a meaningful philosophy of life" 40 percent lower than their counterparts four decades ago. While the article posed interesting research on this up-and-coming group, it also raised questions and got me thinking about the concept of success.

What is success, anyway? What does it mean to be successful? Is the appearance of success, like wealth or fame, the same as being successful? Who is successful and who isn't? And who determines it?

If both wealth and fame are the parameters by which success is to be judged, then Martin Luther King, Jr., Mother Teresa, and Gandhi would not be in the success hall of fame, nor would Susan B. Anthony, Abraham Lincoln, or Rosa Parks. Yet these people positively changed the world with their unique gifts.

So have scores of inventors, teachers, writers, musicians, scientists, designers, builders, doctors, leaders, parents, and engineers. But they weren't rich and famous, and no magazines devoted pages to their day-to-day sightings.

Yet without their achievements, the conveniences we take for granted, the technologies that save our lives, and the endeavors that engage our souls wouldn't exist—accomplishments like airplanes, x-rays, medicines, bridges, Post-it notes, cell phones, movies, music, books, microwaves, computers, prosthetics, fashions, and ATMs, to name but a few.

Every day, people who are bringing themselves to work focus on new ideas, breakthrough technologies, and solutions to global problems. They focus on child rearing, firefighting, and community building. They focus on education, service, and healing. They don't have household names and may struggle to pay the mortgage, but they're successful.

There's a better definition of success, and people who are *hitting their stride* know it. Success is not about money. It's not about recognition or glory or fame. It's not an outward measure someone else establishes. And while money, recognition, and fame may come to people who are *winning at working*, the difference is this: it's not the goal. It's a by-product of their passionate endeavors, hard work, ongoing efforts, and achievements.

For people who are *winning at working*, success is an inner measure of passionately doing what they are able to do, making a difference with their lives, and maximizing their gifts and talents. They measure success by leaving the world a bit better for having been here. That's bringing yourself to work.

Quieting the noise around you, learning about yourself, and discovering your gifts are good places to start. Below are a few ways to begin.

Reflective Exercise: Learning About Yourself

Simple Ways to Ignite Your Connection . . .

Ideas to Quiet the Noise Around You
- On a scale of 1 (never) to 10 (most of the time), rate how often your mind is quiet, still, or calm without critical self-talk, to-do swarms, debilitating second-guessing, or overwhelming emotions. If you score yourself 6 or under, start with five minutes a day of quiet mind. Progress as you master each five-minute increment until you start to hear your voice emerge.
- At least one vacation a year. It can even be a long weekend, but do something for you. Not for your kids or your significant other or your friends or family. Just for you. What location nourishes your soul, calms your stress, or connects your heart? Go there. Take a journal. Take two days to unwind, then write thoughts once a day as they

come to you, without judgment. Don't edit or read what you write, just write. Ask you what you're feeling, thinking, desiring, fearing, hoping?

- Spend time every day outside. It doesn't matter what you do. Walking. Weeding. Playing. Watching. Notice something new every day in nature, growing, emerging, decaying, changing, shining, as if through the eyes of a child. Stop for an instance. Note it. Celebrate it. Feel it. Breathe it. Store its memory.

Ideas to Learn About Yourself

- Pay attention to your intuition and insights. Jot them down. Is there a pattern emerging on how or when you hear your inner voice? If so, start trusting that pattern and acting on nudges coming from inside.
- Pay attention to your disappointments, fears, anger, and frustrations at work. Write them down. What does this tell you? What are your triggers? Feelings? Responses? Now find the watcher in you. Go there. Observe yourself in these moments and ask yourself if you're the one watching or the one doing. What can you learn about you as you are watching?
- Look at work relationships as a chance to learn about yourself. What do you see in the other person that is a mirror for you—positive or not positive? What behaviors in others make you judgmental? Why? Who are you judging?

Ideas to Discover Your Gifts

- Ease and grace, or grind and pain? On a scale of 1 to 10, pay attention when work is easy for you and when it's difficult. When are you fast and accurate, or slow and tedious? What's different about the situation? Note when tasks absorb you, you lose track of time or surroundings. What are you doing when that happens?
- What words do people use to describe you? Write them down. Cross out the ones that don't ring true or sound like they're talking about someone you don't know. Now write the positive words you use to describe yourself. Circle the words in common. *(continued on p. 142)*

(*continued from p. 141*)
- What do your boss or co-workers ask you to do that may not be in your job description, but you've become the go-to person? Why? What are they seeing in you?
- Label four columns: Like to Do in Spare Time, Like to Do at Work, Would Delegate if I Could, Would Like to Be Given to Do at Work. Fill in the columns with specific tasks. What can you learn about your natural talents from this?

HONORING OTHERS' GIFTS

Knowing what your gifts are is only part of the equation. Leveraging what you do well with what others do well is also part of *winning at working*. Learning to recognize, respect, and embrace the unique talents of those you work with or for, including customers, vendors, and suppliers, is key. But I didn't learn that lesson as manager. I learned it as a parent.

One day when I was six, I decided I was special, different, unique from other kids. Quiet and shy, it was something I discerned from watching others and making mental comparisons along the way. I could read better. I could finish my work faster. I could remember all my spelling words. I was even picked first for kickball. I remember the moment vividly. Smugly I decided "yes, I was special."

By twelve, the smugness was long gone. With no abundance of mechanical skills, limited spatial relations, and grace more fitting to after-school softball than ballet lessons, I was envious of the skills I noticed in others. Still I reasoned, you can't have everything. Reinforced by growing academic praise, I mentally tipped the scale in my favor and decided, I was still special.

So it went over the years until our son, Ian, arrived on the scene. His gifts were in art, music, and creative endeavors. I was awed at the things that came easily to him. I was not always patient with the things that didn't. In ninth grade he announced he did not want to be like his parents, and he was not going to college. After Ian's proclamation, reinforced by declining grades, we sought help.

After a few weeks of him attending counseling alone, we were invited. The counselor asked if we were willing to complete a project she had Ian create. The instructions were explicit. We were to work alone, bring our assignments to the next session, and present them to Ian. And we were to do our very best work. Eager to help our son, we agreed. Out came an artistic, but seemingly straightforward, project.

The experience was humbling. I spent hours working on my assignment, frustrated by my inability to translate what I saw in my head. When unveiled to Ian, he laughed. He didn't mean to laugh at my work, he said, but he couldn't believe how bad it was. He explained that he gave me a very easy project. I explained I did my best, and it wasn't easy for me. A wise counselor helped us communicate that day, helping me understand that trying hard doesn't always bring good results, and helping Ian understand our desire was for him to be him, not us. (In case you're curious, today Ian is a successful software development manager and a graduate of Syracuse University with a BFA.)

I will never be artistic, technically inclined, or a good cook. I will never be a lot of things. But I still think I'm special. But now, I know everyone is. Ian taught me that, helping me to see it's not what you can't be, it's what you can be.

Thanks to Ian, I saw workmates with new eyes, watching for their unique gifts and talents and recognizing they were usually different from mine. As a manager, I found what I labeled the "round holes, square pegs" problem. The round talents of people were not best suited for the square tasks they were asked to complete. Yes, they could do the job, but it wasn't a natural fit for their talents.

Progressing to more responsible jobs provided me more opportunity and flexibility to create jobs around people's talents whenever possible, just as jobs were carved out that used my talents. If that can happen, people thrive. When it can't, people struggle doing portions of a job, like I struggled completing Ian's art assignment. *Winning at working* managers find ways to tap into the talents and gifts of their staff.

TEN TIPS FOR HONORING OTHERS' GIFTS AT WORK

1. Weller's Law: "Nothing is impossible for the person who doesn't have to do it."
2. What's easy for you may not be easy for others. That doesn't make you better, just better at that.
3. What's hard for you may not be hard for others. That doesn't make them better than you, just better at that.
4. Find people to work with who love to do what you don't like to do.
5. Create teams or become part of teams, where people have different skills and are valued for using them.
6. Leverage people's strengths; ignore, where possible, their weaknesses.
7. Don't put a higher value on your gifts and talents than someone else's. All are important, depending on what's needed at the time.
8. Recognize you may not see what others see in a co-worker, but that doesn't mean they're not adding value.
9. There are many ways to accomplish the same result, so be open to others' ways to do the work.
10. Look for the uniqueness in other people and help them bring their gifts to the workplace.

Popular in many organizations is a basic understanding of personality types or temperaments using instruments like Myers-Briggs to differentiate natural styles. That's not what I'm talking about here. Honoring others' gifts is not about your style, it's about your uniqueness. One of my gifts is translating concepts for others to "see" or feel or do. One of my father's was writing and playing music from his soul. A good friend can identify trends and generate ideas around them. My husband can turn complex thoughts or problems into simple understandable ones. Each of us has multiple gifts. These are things we do easily, naturally, and exceptionally.

I made plenty of mistakes as a young manager, but not honoring others' gifts was one of my larger ones. I still regret not giving an outstanding rating to an exceptional performer who led a team for a new site opening. At the time, I undervalued her strengths, applying absolute standards of measurement that were impossible to achieve. I wish I'd had Ian's lesson back then.

YOUR WAY

In an episode of *Grey's Anatomy,* two MD rivals for the top job discover after the hospital's surgical chief announced his retirement, that two more had stepped up to vie for the job. It struck me that these doctors threw their stethoscopes in the ring, not necessarily because they wanted the job, but because they were supposed to want the job. In the words of nineteenth-century philosopher Arthur Schopenhauer, "We forfeit three-fourths of ourselves in order to be like other people."

Like the chameleon, we react to the temperature, light, and mood of our environment. Sometimes people, pressure, or stress cause us to respond in a way to fit in, be recognized, or go-along to get-along. Sometimes our responses appear to others like color changes. Our decisions or actions are out of character for us. I've had a few of these in my life. In fact, when I think of the choices I'm least proud of, most stem from chameleon-like behaviors. But unlike the chameleon, some of my color changes lasted for months or even years.

Like taking up cigarette smoking in graduate school because a boyfriend found it sexy. That lasted years past the relationship. Or slowly losing a grounded perspective for what mattered when increased power and influence at work seduced me into a lopsided life. These and other chameleon-esque choices took me away from doing my work, my way, away from my authentic self.

Approaching your work your way is not as simple as these words suggest. You don't order your work or career the way you want it, like a fast-food hamburger. As the saying goes, here's where the rubber meets the road. You can affect your results and performance trust significantly by creating your own luck, seeing the elephant, telling the right stories, and doing a host of other concepts in this book.

But until you step courageously out of the pretend-to-be-box into the this-is-me-box, you won't be *hitting your stride.*

You may appear to be in the eyes of others, but you will know that success achieved not your way is not the success you're seeking. Your heart will not soar, your eyes will not sparkle, and your individual greatness, your "it factor" will not shine. CEO Brian Buffini puts it this way, "Success is usually measured by comparing ourselves to other people. My true goal is significance, which is when we compare ourselves with the gifts that God has given us and our own potential."

After speaking on this topic at a Los Angeles conference, I was answering questions from the stage when a young woman asked, "I know what you're saying. But how do I do that when I'm in a job I don't particularly like, doing work that isn't my strength, surrounded by people that make me crazy?"

What I said to her was this, "This may sound harsh and that's not my intention. But the reality is . . . this is your life. It's the only chance you have to become who you are capable of becoming and bring your uniqueness to the world. Every day you make a choice. There's a difference in doing work you're passionate about, that gets you excited to get up in the morning, and simply having a job. You have to decide which path you want to be on."

Opening on Broadway, Julia Roberts made her debut in *Three Days of Rain.* Prior to opening, the Oscar-winning actress expressed her fear about her theater debut this way, "By the time I get there," Roberts told the *New York Times,* "I'll be entirely apoplectic. But the terror is part of the excitement."

That's not the case for most of us. The terror isn't the excitement that pushes us on but the barrier that holds us back. Too often we default to our fears, letting them reign over life's opportunities. It's fear that decides if we're interested in going for a new position, moving to a new city, changing careers, speaking to groups, or learning new skills. It's fear that hijacks our potential, stifles our growth and constrains us from bringing ourselves to work and *hitting our stride.*

Maybe you're afraid of failure or afraid of success, so you decide it's better to stay with what you know. Maybe you're afraid you'll be disappointed in your results, so you cocoon yourself in your comfort zone. Maybe you're afraid you'll look foolish, so you opt out of competing, or you're concerned you'll be found out as an imposter, or disliked if you pursue your passions, or fail if you step up to more responsibility.

It doesn't matter what your fears are or why you give them control. What matters is if you let them limit you, if you trade your comfort for your relevance, and if you compromise your life's potential to eliminate that pit in your stomach. And if you do, it's no wonder you're not living your dreams.

People who are *winning at working* push past their fears, following the advice of a popular book to "feel the fear and do it anyway." They don't let their fears stop them. They seize their nervous apprehensions and self-limiting concerns, recognizing it takes a little fear to sharpen their skills, push them to the next level, enhance their talents, and maximize their growth. It takes a little fear to dare to become who you are capable of becoming. And it takes a little fear to offer your uniqueness to the world in spite of insecurities, naysayers, and comfort zones.

Of course there are risks in pushing past our fears. We may find our level of incompetence or fail at a new endeavor. But management guru Peter Drucker put it this way, "There is the risk you cannot afford to take and there is the risk you cannot afford not to take." This is the latter.

Determining what your way is requires self-reflection and an investment in peeling your onion of limiting beliefs, chameleon-esque behaviors, fears, comfort-zone boundaries, strengths, and limitations. It requires discovering not only who you are, but also who you are not. These are not topics for one chapter in one book. But the following box contains a few concepts to consider along the way:

REFLECTIVE THINKING EXERCISE: YOUR WAY AT WORK

On a scale of 1 to 5, rate yourself.

1 = Never 2 = Rarely 3 = Sometimes
4 = Usually 5 = Almost Always

1. I say "yes" at work when I could and want to say "no."
2. When I disagree with the work, I offer my opinion.
3. I need to compromise my values and integrity to do my work.
4. I look forward to Mondays.
5. My work uses my unique skills and abilities.
6. I think that if my boss knew what I was capable of doing, he'd be surprised.
7. I like who I am at work—the "me" I show the world.
8. My work is what I do, not who I am.
9. I feel like I'm following my dreams.
10. I like the work I do and know that it's well-suited to my talents.
11. My performance review confirms I'm using my strengths at work.
12. I have the courage to stick to my principles at work.
13. I feel my job has changed me more than I'd like.
14. I put me on my priority life list.
15. I live up to other people's expectations.
16. I live up to my own expectations.
17. I want to fit in and please others.
18. My work life is stress and grind.
19. My work life is ease and grace.
20. I offer the best of who I am at work.

Self-Assessment Scoring
If you scored *more* than 65 points, you are, more often than not, finding your way at work. If you scored *less* than 65, you may want to pay attention to the decisions and work moments that feel unauthentic to you. Once you start to recognize when you are not showing up, you can choose a different outcome. Then revisit this list in three or four months and note the progress you're making.

I've been on this journey toward authentic self for a while now, and I know it's not a straight path. Some weeks or months or years, I'm more grounded in who I am and my work, my way, than other weeks or months or years. There are setbacks, obstacles, soul-depleting environments, stressful life happenings, and drifting sands that impede the way. But being on the path is better than not in this journey of becoming.

By working in whatever individual ways work for you and hearing the messages that seem to speak only to you, you can grow, develop, change, and evolve because you want to. That's what I'm suggesting here. Finding and offering your gifts and honoring the gifts of others are first steps. Approaching your work, your way, requires a deeper commitment to your life's potential.

Eleanor Roosevelt punctuates the messages in this chapter with these words, "Remember always that you have not only the right to be an individual; you have an obligation to be one. You cannot make any useful contribution in life unless you do this."

8

A PRACTICE OF TRUST

"I would rather be the man who bought the Brooklyn Bridge than the one who sold it." **Will Rogers**

Living in the population-challenged state of Montana, it's a treat to go shopping on business trips. Excited about the prospect, I planned to do just that at a large mall in suburban Philadelphia. Prepared to put more than miles on my American Express card, my first stop was a nationally known department store. After forty minutes selecting outfits, I was eager to narrow the choices.

Arms aching with clothes, I met a locked fitting-room door. I tried the next door. Locked. All the doors to all fitting rooms were locked. "I'll find a person with a key," I confidently thought, despite no sales associates in sight. I walked the department. I walked the adjacent department. No one. Returning to the department, I waited while no one came. After twenty minutes, I left potential purchases of over eleven hundred dollars piled on the register stand and walked out.

While I may be sympathetic to budget and staffing challenges, I'm not sympathetic to the customer message I received. This retailer spends millions in advertising enticing me into its store. But once I'm there, they don't trust me, their customer, not to steal from them? I know it's not the personal me, but the generic one.

It's a sad commentary when a national department store has to lock its fitting room doors because too many people steal from them. Society is a reflection of the people who comprise it. It's a collective indictment on who we are, what we do, and what we value or don't value. My shopping experience mirrored today's shattered trust. It got me thinking.

When we denounce looters who steal, but help ourselves to office supplies from our employers, we share in the accountability of dishonesty. When we buy a child's ticket at a theme park when our child is past the age restriction, we model to our children it's okay to "lie a little," and we share in the accountability when they grow up and they do. When our word or our handshake is not as good as a contract, we lose ground with those we give it to, and we share in the accountability of broken promises.

Why aren't we surprised to learn from the *New York Times* that the head of the IRS says it's losing the war on tax cheats? Or outraged to read in the *Washington Post* that 74 percent of high school students, in a survey of 4,500, admitted to cheating on a big test? It's not okay with us that our corporate leaders cheat, filling courtrooms for their misdeeds and greed. But it's okay that our children do? That we do?

When did it become acceptable to embellish resumes, cherry-pick term papers from the Internet, and fabricate stories? When did the *win* become more important than *how* we achieved it?

Trust is not about *them* in corporate or political America; it's about *us* in everyday America. So it's no surprise that our workplaces offer another view of the same picture. Consider these examples:

★ Fifty-six percent of resumes "contain falsehoods of some kind," according to a *New York Times* columnist. One resume in the headlines was David J. Edmondson's. Former chief executive of Radio-Shack, Mr. Edmondson resigned after news of his resume embellishment was revealed, fabricating two college degrees when he had zero.

★ Sixty-three percent of employees admit calling out sick when they're not, a *Reader's Digest* survey notes.

★ According to an American management survey: 76 percent of employers monitor employee Internet use, 55 percent keep and review employee e-mail messages, 51 percent use video surveillance, 31 percent monitor outgoing phone calls. Personally, I'd suggest instead, the Chinese proverb, "If you suspect a man, don't employ him, and if you employ him, don't suspect him."

★ Ever tell your significant other you paid less for an item than you did? Ever pad your expense account? According to a survey for CNNMoney.com, 71 percent of participants admitted to lying about money or keeping money secrets.

★ Since 1983, Duluth, Minnesota, offered "free lifetime health care to all of its retired workers, their spouses and children up to age 26." Twenty-two years later the mayor admits, "There was not a nickel set aside." Headlines remind us that Duluth is not the only employer under-funding promises to employees.

Now that skepticism has turned to cynicism about everyone from politicians to priests, how do we build back the trust? When, according to American Demographics, more people trust infomercials and used-car salesmen than company leaders, how do we reengage the trust of those we work with? How do we reengage our own? And what is trust, anyway?

That's what this chapter is about. You'll consider what workplace trust is and isn't, ascertain how to transform work results using trust, and find tips, insights, and practical ways to enhance trust building. You'll discover why *winning at working* means developing a personal practice of trust. And perhaps you'll ascertain what I did: trust is another way. As Jack R. Gibb puts it, "Trust opens the doorway to the spirit."

THE NEW CURRENCY

The call for another way is almost palpable. We are on the

cusp of an era where trust will become the new workplace currency. Partially it will happen because we don't have any choice in this world where intellectual property is the competitive edge, and innovative solutions are needed for both companies and countries. And partially it will happen because we do have a choice to change our direction, and we will.

Gallup polling confirms what most of us see in our workplaces: 70 percent of us are disengaged. Disengaged employees keep their ideas quiet and their discretionary efforts tamed. While the company that signs our check can buy our presence on the job, they can't crowbar ideas from our head or engage our passions for work.

We live in a world where it's hard to differentiate a real photograph from one created by computer wizardry, and advertising language has complicated even the simple choice of beverage size, so it's no wonder people find it hard to trust the messages. When corporate leaders are escorted handcuffed from courtrooms, and thousands lose their jobs as a result of corporate greed and misdeeds, it's no wonder people find it hard to trust the messengers.

But there is another way, a better way, a more soul-filled way, and most of us know it. In this new era, company-driven ways will be replaced by authentic practices driven by individuals. This twenty-first-century business culture will not be marked by aligned cultures or the value-driven companies of the '90s, although such practices certainly provide solid foundations. Instead, it will be an era marked by individual choice.

Each of us—by showing up as who we are capable of being—will create, shepherd, and transform our workplaces. The world needs what we have to give. Offering our ideas, our engagement, and our unique gifts matters on two levels: first, living our life's potential, and second, contributing to the creation of a better world.

WHAT TRUST IS AND ISN'T

There's a story frequently told in training classes about a man named Zumbrati. It goes something like this: Zumbrati finished a harrowing tightrope walk across Niagara Falls. Nearly losing his footing when a wind gust struck, the famous aerialist was happy to be on firm footing. As he reached the bank, one fan was waiting with a wheelbarrow. "Wow, that was great," the fan told Zumbrati, "but I know you can do it again pushing this wheelbarrow."

Shaking his head, Zumbrati said he felt lucky to have made it across at all. "Oh, you can do it," persisted the man. "Please, just give it a try with the wheelbarrow." Again Zumbrati shook his head. The nagging fan pressed. Again and again he pushed for another try. In desperation, Zumbrati responded, "I guess you really believe in me, don't you?"

"Oh yes," exclaimed the fan. "I know you can do it."

"Well then," said Zumbrati, "we'll do it together. Get in the wheelbarrow."

Some say this story is about trust. For many, it even illustrates their definition of the word. While it is a story about trust, Zumbrati and his fan illustrate what's called simple, blind, or naive trust—the kind a child has for a parent. But it's not the trust that transforms lives. It's not the trust that builds organizational cultures. And it's not the trust discussed in this chapter. Let me be clear with my definition—in the context of this book, I'm referring to authentic trust.

Most of us think we know what trust is and isn't. But trust is the most misunderstood word at work, resulting in perceptions of broken promises and trampled expectations. If you ask five friends, you'll likely get five definitions. People mean different things when they use the word, often interchanging it with words like "reliable" or "predictable" or "trustworthy."

See what you know about this misunderstood word, "trust."

**REFLECTIVE THINKING EXERCISE:
WHAT IS AUTHENTIC TRUST ANYWAY?**

True or False
1. The opposite of trust is mistrust. (*continued on p. 156*)

(*continued from p. 155*)

2. Trust is unconditional.
3. It is always good to trust.
4. You can trust things as well as people.
5. Once trust has been betrayed, it cannot be recovered.
6. Trust is about making and honoring commitments.
7. Trust is about building relationships.
8. Trust is a choice.
9. Trust is an emotional skill that requires judgment.
10. Trust is not something that can be learned.
11. Trust is what holds organizations, groups, and people together.
12. Trust involves mindful integrity.
13. Self-trust is the most neglected form of trust.
14. Trust is an ongoing process.
15. Risk is part of trust.
16. To get trust, you must earn it.
17. Once you've established trust, you can forget about it.
18. Being trusted typically increases self-confidence and self-respect.
19. Trust is based on reliance and predictability.
20. People are wired to trust.

Self-Assessment Scoring
The questions numbered 6, 7, 8, 9, 12, 13, 14, 15, 18, and 20 are true. The remaining questions are false.

If I'd taken this quiz at the beginning or middle of my career, I would have missed the majority of questions. But as I've evolved to offer a more authentic self to the world (warts and all), my trust understanding has morphed and grown from basic to authentic. Here's a few misunderstandings I've encountered:

Ten Misunderstood Truths About Trust

1. What people often think is trust, is not. Unsophisticated optimism illustrated in the story about Zumbrati and his fan is not authentic trust.

It's unsophisticated, unthinking, unreflective, and naive. While it's the basic trust that most of us start with as babies, many adults still hold to that simple orientation of the world. Childlike trust operates without acknowledging any potential of distrust. It's not realistic or authentic.

2. Trust is about people, not things.

   Trust involves interpersonal engagement. We use the word, associating trust with things as well as people, but one can't really "trust" their car. We confuse trust with dependable or reliable, both in relation to things and people. Trust requires commitments made and commitments honored. It necessitates deliberate decisions, action, and response.

3. Trust is not always a good thing.

   Trust is not inherently good or not good. It's how it's applied. Non-authentic trust can be naive, foolish, or blind. Blind trust involves self-deception and denial. It is unshakeable and closed to the possibility of betrayal. Yet betrayal is a risk of trust.

4. Trust is conditional.

   Trust is not a blank check. There are limits and conditions. When we say we trust someone, there is a presumed statement of conditionality. For example, while I may trust my mechanic to work on my car, I wouldn't trust him to do my root canal.

5. Trust can be regained once betrayed or broken.

   Like virginity, simple trust cannot be regained. But that's not the case with authentic trust. Authentic trust is not black or white, but operates in shades of grey. Authentic trust is focused more on the relationship than on a particular outcome. It is open to rebuilding, keeping in perspective what matters for the relationship.

6. Mistrust is not the opposite of trust.

   The opposite of trust is control. Notice where there is a lack of authentic trust, and you'll see control. Giving trust is a choice to be made, but once it is given, freedom with accountability is at its core.

7. Trust is a process.

Trust is an action. It is not an atmosphere or a glue that holds things together. It's not a screensaver that waits in the background until it's needed. It's something we consciously do as individuals. Trust is an ongoing process of relationship building. It's an emotional skill that is learned.

8. Self-trust is part of trust.

Self-trust is trusting your own intentions, motives, and integrity. It's meeting your expectations and keeping your word. It involves self-esteem and self-confidence. If you can't trust yourself, how can you trust someone else? If you don't trust yourself to behave with ethics or integrity in a situation, you'll find it hard to trust that others would. We assume people are like us. If we're deceitful, we think others are, too. If we're trustworthy, we look at others that way.

9. There is risk with trust.

Authentic trust doesn't deny what has happened in the past or ignore the possibility of future betrayal, intentional or unintentional. It understands there is the possibility of a breech of trust, and weighs risks and benefits before proceeding. Authentic trust is action developed through critical thought and experience.

10. To get trust, you must give it.

Contrary to popular belief, you do not get trust because you earn it. You get it because you give it. It's the law of reciprocity: you get what you give. If you want to be trusted, you must first trust. While some think that's counterintuitive, it's not. It's no different from other relationship processes. You get love, not by being loveable, but by loving. You get information not by hoarding, but by sharing. You get respect by respecting others. Trust is no different.

We're even wired for trust. Emery University research was summarized in the *New York Times* this way: "Hard as it may be to believe in these days of infectious greed and sabers unsheathed, scientists have discovered that the small, brave act of cooperating with another person, of choosing trust over cynicism, generosity over selfishness, makes the brain light up with quiet joy."

"Trust isn't something we 'have,' or a medium or an atmosphere within which we operate. Trust is something we do, something we make," according to Robert Solomon and Fernando Flores in *Building Trust in Business, Politics, Relationships, and Life.* Trust is an action. It's a way of operating. You make a significant difference in your workgroup culture when you choose to practice authentic trust. Giving and cultivating authentic trust is a *winning at working* philosophy.

TRUST BROKEN

Sometimes we make mistakes. Sometimes things don't work out. Sometimes matters happen outside of our control that cause commitments not to be honored. Disappointment? Yes. Diminished trust? Maybe. But what happens if we never planned to honor our commitments? What then?

Of all the behaviors negatively affecting trust building in the workplace, lying tops the list of what people say when they think of trust betrayed. According to Solomon and Flores, "Lying embodies a wholesale insincerity—stating as truth what one fully knows not to be true—and may also manifest a profound lack of caring, even when the lie (a 'white lie') is intended to protect the feelings of the person to whom the lie is told. But it is a shortsighted, limited notion of care and may cause violence to the longer-term relationship. ('If you would lie to me about a little thing, how in the world can I ever know when to believe you?'). But many lies are not so white, and not intended to protect the feelings of the recipient. They're rather designed to protect the liar from the consequences of his or her action."

Pain accompanies broken trust, and I've had my share. If I told you the story specifics, you'd understand my lingering anger, disappointment, and hurt. But this is not a woe-is-me section so here's but a glimpse: How about a builder who billed us for work completed, but didn't pay suppliers or subcontractors with our funds? Even after he went to jail, my rage continued. How about a boss dangling the carrot of a big promotion and then hiring the position from the outside without informing me I was out of the running? That dangling carrot did more than wilt. It fueled a sense of betrayal. Or what about the co-worker who I considered a friend? In a moment of workplace stress, I confided in her, only to hear my words come back from my boss. We all have stories we could share where we've offered our trust, only to have it broken.

For part of my life, I operated under a naive basic trust definition. The outcome for me was black or white; I either trusted you or I didn't. You lived up to that trust or you didn't. It took me decades to discover authentic trust and its power to transform relationships and work cultures.

Trust doesn't happen because you want it to happen. It doesn't happen when others are "good enough," "dependable enough," or "trustworthy enough" for us to give them our trust. Despite common thinking, people don't earn our trust. If you work for a boss who believes everyone is out for herself or you can't trust anyone, it's unlikely that person could ever trust you, no matter how trustworthy you are.

Trust is given, not earned. Yet authentic trust is given with intelligent judgment. So because you are trustworthy, there's a higher probability that trust will be given to you. While trust always comes with the possibility of being broken, just like love comes with the possibility of heartbreak, not loving or not trusting diminishes relationships, results, and life experiences.

I remember the first time my heart was broken over trusting. I was eleven. One day we were inseparable best friends. The next day, I locked myself in my bedroom refusing her calls. And even though we played together a few weeks later, it was never the same. She betrayed me. At least, to my fifth-grade way of thinking, she did.

She'd promised me. She told me I was the one she was

inviting to accompany her family to their rented beach house over spring break. Each of her siblings could bring one friend, and I was her choice. Excited about the trip, I nagged my parents until they gave me permission to go. But her invitation never came. I learned of her betrayal from the friend she did invite.

That childhood incident should be long forgotten. But it's still here. Even though I've had significant broken-trust incidents with more life impact, forty-something years later, I can still get to that painful eleven-year-old hurt. It's next to the pain residue of other heart-trespassers, sometimes festering, breaking-open, or boiling-up.

It's funny how we hold on to our pain. It's like picking off a scab on an almost healed cut, waiting until it bleeds a bit before we stop. When my eighty-four-year-old mother was visiting, it was unhealed pain that emerged in her stories, not her days of love and happiness. She got me thinking. What pain am I holding on to that's decreasing my life's joy and happiness? How about you?

Life's emotional events are like touching a cactus. The needles stick us; a few even lodge in our skin. Yet if we pull out the thorns soon after it happens, the wound starts to heal. If we don't, the sliver can work itself deep into our skin. So every time we bump it, it hurts. That's what happened to me. I let those emotional cactus needles burrow into my heart.

At the time, I wasn't good at dealing with my emotions when something painful happened. Sometimes, I deliberately buried them, hoping the pain would disappear. Sometimes, I pushed them away, not feeling emotionally strong enough to work through my feelings. And sometimes, I refused to acknowledge that it even hurt. I let those emotional needles burrow into my life, creating heartsores. And while the years covered them with scar tissue, they didn't completely heal, flaring up, or getting infected by similar feelings, thoughts, or events.

I finally realized, you can't live life without getting a few cactus needles along the way. But what you do about it makes all the difference. Now I know to face my emotions when hurt happens, not allow them to take up residence in my heart. It's better to work through disappointment, broken promises, and diminished trust up front than let it dig its way into your future.

SELF-TRUST

You can't have a practice of trust without including yourself in that endeavor. Ralph Waldo Emerson claims, "Self-trust is the first secret of success." I think he's right. But I would add it's the ongoing secret, too. Self-trust is "the ability to trust oneself to trust wisely and authentically," according to Solomon and Flores.

Do you trust you? Can you trust your motives, intentions, impulses and judgment? Do you lie to yourself? Do you break promises you make to yourself? Can you count on you to deliver what you say you will? Are you in an authentic relationship with yourself? Do you trust your judgment and risks taken when giving trust? Lack of self-trust can be the precursor of distrusting others. It's hard to trust others if you don't trust yourself.

Self-trust goes deeper. Self-trust grows the inner path and aids discovery of your life's potential. Author Jack R. Gibb puts it this way, "Trust creates the flow and gentles the mind-body-spirit. When I trust myself I am able to enter fully into the process of discovering and creating who I am. When I trust my own inner processes I am able to become what I am meant to become."

The most important relationship you can have is with yourself. A practice of authentic trust offers you a way to explore your possibilities, your gifts, and your soul's desire.

CREATE YOUR POCKET OF EXCELLENCE

People work for people, not for companies. No one needs permission to create his or her own pocket of excellence. Trust is not about them giving it to us. Trust is an action we can take. We start trust by giving trust.

I agree with Booker T. Washington, who said, "Few things help an individual more than to place responsibility upon him, and to let him know that you trust him." I agree with

Mr. Washington because I've experienced trust. I've been on both the giving and receiving side of the equation, and I know firsthand its power.

That's what trust is. Power. Power to transform an ordinary, everyday, okay place to work into an environment where people are almost unstoppable. Power to unleash creativity, commitment, enthusiasm, and fun. Power to bring out the energy, talents, and gifts of individuals, to build teams, to achieve amazing results. Power to unleash the gifts of the soul.

Look around your organization. There's some division or department or work unit or team that's like that—some pocket of excellence where people shine, ideas flourish, and exceptional work is achieved; some soul-enhancing place where extraordinary is ordinary, and people feel free to show up, in the fullest sense of the word, with their unique gifts and talents. That's where trust is.

But even simple behaviors can diminish it. The first question I ask when a staff member shows up in my office to tell a tale of woe about a co-worker is: "Have you talked to her?" I can count on one hand how many times in twenty years of managing I heard "yes." Ninety-nine percent of the time, the person who is the offending party was never told about the issue before it was escalated to management. Will the co-worker feel betrayed? I did when a peer went to my boss without giving me a chance to address his concerns, or informing me there even was an issue. Was trust diminished? You can bet on that one.

Hate those e-mails where someone cc'd "the world," including your boss and your boss's boss, and everyone else's boss? Not a trust-building behavior, I'd say. What can you do about it? Don't send e-mails like that and don't push the "reply all" button. Address your remarks to those who need to be included versus covering your you-know-what.

Ever get irritated when people blow off meetings, miss deadlines, and take weeks to reply? Not behaviors that build trust. Be aware of behaviors that irritate you, and don't do them. Model the behaviors you want from others.

If you want to work in a trusting environment, pay

attention to yourself and to your thinking, your intentions, your actions, your commitments, and your promises. Trust is not blind or unconditional, and it's not without risk. But it is a powerful choice you can make if you want to be *winning at working.*

So, what's it worth to work in a pocket of excellence that's fueled by trust? John Helliwell and Haifang Huang put a monetary number on that question. These University of British Columbia economists analyzed surveys identifying four factors in job satisfaction. They learned that an increased trust in management produced satisfaction levels equivalent to a 36 percent salary increase. Likewise, decreasing trust levels in management caused a satisfaction decline equal to a 36 percent pay cut.

It's no surprise that Watson Wyatt's WorkUSA survey discovered companies without trust are paying on the bottom-line: "The three-year total return to shareholders is almost three times lower at companies with low trust levels than companies with high trust levels." And Great Places to Work Institute states on its websites, "Trust between managers and employees is the primary defining characteristic of the best workplaces."

You knew that, didn't you? Most working adults have firsthand experience that trust enhances the workplace, and broken promises, hypocrisy, manipulation, and lies negatively affect engagement, commitment, performance, and the bottom-line.

You may not be able to change your boss's behavior or the bosses above her, but you can influence the environment of those you work with and those who work for you. You can create your own pocket of excellence, and in the process, give the equivalent of a 36 percent pay increase to others by a practice of trust. So the question is, how do you do that? In the next section, you'll find suggestions, insights, and ideas to help you develop your practice of trust.

YOUR PRACTICE OF TRUST

Since you want to be *winning at working* by offering the best of who you are to your work, then developing a practice of trust is paramount. There are three keys to trust building. They're not a magic formula nor all inclusive. They are, however, foundational pieces, cornerstones as it were. But let me give you the bottom-line to all three: authentic trust comes from authentic people.

Three Keys to Building Trust

Key #1: Give It First

Stories of intrigue, treachery, politics, lies, double crosses, and power struggles fill the history books, much like they fill today's headlines. In the world of the seventeenth-century musketeer, one's life depended on who you could trust. In the world of the twenty-first-century employee, one's livelihood may.

I'm not naive to organizational politics, competition, or sabotage in the workplace. I've held my own in companies where silos, turf wars, and power brokers delivered indigestion, sleepless nights, and distrusting cultures. But I still don't get it. When people are more focused on what's happening in the cube next to them than on achieving company goals, everyone loses. When company politics fill e-mails with mixed direction, stalling productivity, everyone loses. And when discretionary effort and new ideas are swallowed in pits of bureaucracy, guess what? Everyone loses. The way I see it, if the company fails, we all fail.

So, I believe *The Three Musketeers* got it right: "All for one and one for all!" Each understood that his fate as an individual was tied to their fate as a group. Trusting each other was unambiguous. One was in trouble, they all were in trouble. One needed help, they all provided help. One succeeded, they all succeeded. The fiction of Alexandre Dumas, set in the seventeenth century, seems a good prescription for the twenty-first-century century workplace.

I know it's worked for me. Arriving at a new job, I discovered the boss who hired me was away, and no one expecting me. I found no office, no desk, and no information. The person I was hired to replace was in my job and had no idea I was replacing her. Each week got worse.

Information and requests flowed like water through a clogged pipe. I was out of the loop on important issues and viewed as the enemy. Turning to my boss for guidance was like stepping into a sinkhole as I discovered his credibility and that of the department both lacking.

I realized if I was to survive, I had to find, win over, and/or develop a handful of people I could trust. It took a difficult year, but the payoff lasted an entire career. Gradually the group of trusted colleagues grew. We never thought of ourselves as musketeers, but by our actions, we became them. Unspoken rules of ethics and integrity prevailed. We looked beyond individual interests. We shared ideas, collaborated on projects, borrowed resources, and worked together easily and enthusiastically. We wanted the best for each other and the best for the company, each of us worrying about more than our five acres.

Unspoken commitments prevailed. If I was in trouble or asked for help, help was given. I was called upon to step up and provide help, too. We all knew our musketeer roles required reciprocity. The bottom-line was that helping each other to succeed, helped each of us succeed. I don't know where I'd be today without the musketeer approach. And it all started by giving trust, because in order to get trust, I had to give it first.

What I learned from the musketeers about trust is this: relationships are paramount. In times of desperation, corporate politics, near impossible deadlines, organizational changes, confusion, and defeat, it's the relationships that sustain us and get us through. It's the relationships that build pockets of excellence. It's the relationships that create soul-enhancing workplaces. And it's authentic trust that builds those relationships.

Think of trust not as a light switch but a dimmer. When the dimmer switch is on low, there's a little light. Giving trust is like that. You start on low. Early in a new work relationship, you might say. "Run it by me first." Then, as you give more trust, moving from low to medium, it's more like, "Keep me posted on what you're doing." Followed by a higher trust level: "Let me know if you get into trouble."

A practice of trust is a practice of relationship building.

That vision enables you to make the right long-term decisions. By making the relationship primary, tasks and outcomes take care of themselves.

Key #2: Show Up

There is transparency with authentic people. I think of them as WYSIWYG (pronounced wiz-ee-wig) people. It's a term used by software developers for what-you-see-is-what-you-get. WYSIWYG allows a developer to see what the end result will look like during the development process. For example, there's a WYSIWYG editor with my blog (www.nanrussell.com/blog) so I can preview before I publish it to the site. The same concept applies to people.

Authentic, WYSIWYG people, don't surprise you. They don't lie to you. They don't manipulate you. They don't deceive you. They don't deliberately mislead you. They're not hypocritical. They aren't trying to be anyone but who they are, so they're what-you-see-is-what-you-get people. You'll know when they're angry or frustrated, excited or stressed, irritable or compassionate. They're genuine, credible, good-to-their-word people who authentically show up.

There's nothing perfect about them. They have strengths and weaknesses like everyone else. But unlike most of us, they're not trying to copy others. They're only trying to be who they are. Authentic people are not saint-like, but self-like.

When you "show up," you change the work dynamic. You raise the bar for yourself and others by putting skin in the game, setting the expectation for how to operate, and expecting nothing less from others in return. When you speak and act from conviction, well-intentioned thought, and winning philosophies, others follow your lead. When you contribute trust, others offer it as well.

REFLECTIVE THINKING EXERCISE: ARE YOU SHOWING UP?

Personal insight is more likely if you write your answers.

1. Describe who you are at home, at work, and at play. Are there differences and if so, what might that tell you about you? (*continued on p. 168*)

(*continued from p. 167*)

2. Do you ever find yourself apologizing for who you are? If so, why?

3. How easy is it for you to stick to your principles? What causes you to lose your grounding?

4. When you look in the mirror, do you recognize the eyes behind the mask? Describe the person looking out at you. Is that who you are at work?

5. Describe the uniqueness that is you. Would people at work describe you in the same way?

6. Do you know that place where you are the watcher, watching you? If so, who do you see when you watch yourself at work? Is that you or who you think you're supposed to be?

7. When you grow old, will you look back and think, "I could have been me," or "I played the music in my soul?" Does that change anything?

8. How has your work changed who you are? Or has it? Positively or negatively?

9. If you consider your intentions behind your workplace actions, are they publishable on your company's Intranet?

10. Are you happy with the person you are becoming at work? Why or why not?

Key #3: Communicate

Creating an ongoing process of timely, open communication, centered on dialogue, is the last key. How you see information sharing enhances or blocks your efforts at building trusting relationships. It's like the industrious black-tailed ground squirrel who has his home beneath a stump not far from my office window. I watch him squirrel away provisions, and he reminds me of people I've worked with.

Starting his journey by standing tall on the stump, the squirrel hurriedly looks side to side. When he's certain it's safe, he leaps into the grass, jumping then running to a group of nuts nestled beneath a medium-size pine. There he briefly pauses to make his choice. Selecting one pine nut in his teeth, he darts back to the stump with a run-jump motion. Once again standing tall, he looks for competitors or predators before quickly popping his prized provision into his nest and beginning the process all over again.

Like that squirrel, people often hide what they consider important to their survival at work. It's called information. Hoarding bits and pieces, they act as if information alone is a life-sustaining nutrient. The more information nuggets they have, the safer or more powerful they think they'll be. And while those nuggets might help someone survive in a company culture where information is a bartered commodity, long term it won't help them thrive. Here's why.

They're locked in old thinking about power and success, seeing them as the ability to render authority or influence over someone or something. They think information gives them control. But rules are changing. People don't trust people who want to control them, who want to hoard what's needed for everyone's survival, or who play a company game where there can be just one or two winners. People withhold their ideas and discretionary efforts in cultures like that.

The new power emerging in the work realm is trust. Trust is critical in an era where intellectual property heralds company success. But to build trust, information must be shared. Shared information multiplies as the Italian proverb reminds us: "All the brains are not in one head." People who are *winning at working* realize lighting the next candle doesn't diminish the flame of the original one, and information is critical in lighting ideas, opening possibilities, and creating new horizons for themselves and their companies.

If you want to be *winning at working*, realize your power is in trusting and doing, not in just knowing, and certainly not in hoarding. Trust builds a larger universe of relationships where a big idea comes from two smaller ones, a shared problem brings imaginative solutions, and a common vision produces uncommon results. Like the carbon atom that has the capacity to form charcoal or diamonds, so do you. You will create more work diamonds operating with trust and eliminating the squirrel effect. But that means you have to communicate.

Like love, trust is cultivated, grown, and nurtured. We make authentic trust. We make it by what we do and how we do it. We make it by what we say and how we say it. We make it by showing up and being authentic. We make it by giving it away. We are in the mirror of the world we live in. So, if you don't like the workplace you see, help make a better one.

9

SHADES OF GREY

"Life isn't always black and white."
Paperweight on author's desk

Perhaps I'm not the ideal person to write this chapter. Still, my mental quarreling yielded a decision. It's precisely because I've struggled with absolute thinking that my insights and personal learning may be helpful. After all, it's the former addict who best understands the struggle. As a recovering absolute thinker, I know my perspective is important to share.

A gift from my husband fifteen years ago, the paperweight noted above sits on my desk as a tangible reminder to fight the tendency, especially when upset, angry, or stressed, to view issues as binary: black or white, right or wrong, good or bad, ethical or unethical. When examined thoughtfully, few issues land in either-or buckets. They are more complex, more heart engaging, and more involved than that simple sort allows. They are more human.

In the workplace, absolute thinking limits perspective, causes mistakes in judgment, misunderstandings, disappointments, conflicts, and frustration. Most work issues are not black or white, right or wrong, win or lose. They are varying shades of grey. Adjusting one's blinders to see grey, and adjusting one's heart to hear the person behind the issue, is a *winning at working* philosophy.

Eleanor Roosevelt captures what I've come to understand: *"A mature person is one who does not think only in absolutes, who is able to be objective even when deeply stirred emotionally, who has learned that there is both good and bad in all people and in all things, and who walks humbly and deals charitably with the circumstances of life, knowing that in this world no one is all-knowing and therefore all of us need both love and charity."*

NOT BLACK OR WHITE

Etched in silver with the message, "Life isn't always black and white," my paperweight suggests what I've come to know—there are few absolutes at work or in life. Yet, it would be easier if good ideas from bad, trustworthy people from non-trustworthy, and right paths from the wrong ones could easily be discerned. I've learned increasing one's perspective, knowledge, understanding, and compassion increases the grey, as words like *always* and *never* become obsolete for describing most situations and most people.

But early in my career, I was convinced there were right ways and wrong ways to do things at work. Of course, my way being right and someone else's wrong. Dug in positions that at the time seemed immensely important strike me now as limited in knowledge, understanding, or point of view.

Now I'm as convinced there are multiple ways to accomplish the same goal and many answers to the same problem. Certainly, some approaches are better than others, but whose interpretation defines better? Is on time and on budget a better result than enhanced quality? Maybe. Maybe not. It's a subjective workplace, after all, with complicated intertwined objectives, personalities, and obligations.

It's a matter of judgment if an idea is a good one, a performance rating accurate, or a decision correct. Sometimes interpretation is based on quarterly profits, employee morale, company goals, personal filters, necessity, or a passionate champion embracing a challenge.

That subjective element often frustrates. Some want a playbook or a standard method to judge an outcome so everyone agrees it's good or bad. Yet we have differing vantage points, information, and criteria depending on our roles. There may be big-picture, long-term, short-term, temporary, personal, best, best-of-worst, and more on a long list of considerations.

I learned this as I debated my boss over a decision he was about to implement. As a human resources director, I was concerned the decision would impact morale. HR was the filter by which I judged work at the time. He gently closed the discussion agreeing with my viewpoint, "Yes, it's true employees will be unhappy. But they'll be unhappier if there are layoffs next year. My job is to make sure everyone has a job."

If you want to be *winning at working*, adjust your eyes to see more grey and adjust your beliefs to understand, for the most part, people are doing what they believe to be right, for reasons they believe are right. If we could stand behind them and see what they see, we might even come to the same conclusion.

Half my career I spent in human resources offering guidance on workplace issues, rendering judgment on employee-relations problems, influencing people-friendly thinking in managers, and making decisions on people assets. The other half I spent starting corporate departments, designing culture initiatives, and launching a subsidiary with profit-and-loss accountability.

It was this contrast in experiencing support and line roles that forced me to critique my advice, given so confidently while in human resources. As my responsibility got broader, my perspective larger, and the stakes more significant, former black-and-white issues became multiple shades of grey. Here are a few examples:

BLACK-OR-WHITE THINKING	SHADES OF GREY THINKING
Taking away or reducing employee benefits is a bad management decision.	Difficult decisions are part of management; if the company fails, everyone fails.

(continued on p. 174)

(*continued from p. 173*)

BLACK-OR-WHITE THINKING	SHADES OF GREY THINKING
Employees are the company's most important asset.	Depends. There are many important assets; e.g., no customers, no cash flow.
We need to stay within policy to be fair to everyone.	Sometimes there are reasons to make exceptions; fair is not the same as equal.
Employees will not like the decision.	Work is not a democracy.
It's important to provide training and development for employees.	Maybe, but self-motivated people will figure it out; and where's the ROI?
People need to know what's happening and be told the truth.	Communication is a balance between the needs of people and needs of company.
The best people should always rise to the top.	What is "best?" There are lots of business reasons people get promoted.
Not all your employees can be top performers.	Forced ranking works on paper—not with exceptional teams.

BLACK-OR-WHITE THINKING	SHADES OF GREY THINKING
People should be treated the same; perks for management are unbalanced.	People don't perform the same or have the same accountabilities or pressures.
Focus should be on employee competencies.	It's not what I can do—it's what I actually do.
People need a work-family balance.	Yes, they do, but it's up to me to figure out what that means for my life.
We need to take care of our employees.	Companies are not parents; they need to provide interesting work and opportunity.
We should promote from within, giving current people opportunities to advance.	Absolutely if it makes sense. But there are times when it doesn't for the business.

BLACK-OR-WHITE THINKING	SHADES OF GREY THINKING
That's against company policy.	Maybe the policy is wrong.
We can hire the best people within salary guidelines.	Sometimes companies have to hire the best people no matter the guidelines.
Whatever gets rewarded gets done.	Yes, but often it's not what people think.

Absolute thinking is, well, absolute. It's unmitigated, unconditional, and unqualified. Contracts, laws, regulations, statutes, and specific documents use language to expedite consistent interpretation or decision making within more right-wrong-yes-no parameters. So if your 401(k) program requires twelve months of continuous service prior to enrollment, you'll know the answer if you're a nine-month employee.

But people issues, business decisions, and relationships are not as easy. If your company's salary guidelines preclude you from hiring the right person needed to improve business in a critical job, an exception might be made. Is that fair? To whom? The company? Other employees? How you balance those competing issues, let go of your attachment to a specific outcome, and operate outside a black-white thinking mode influences not only your results, but also how you're perceived by those with more power, influence, and authority, as well as co-workers and staff.

In some companies, limited absolute perspective is called "non-exempt thinking." Of course, the concept doesn't apply exclusively or categorically to hourly employees, but is shorthand to describe people, at all levels, who based on their precise perspective, limited experience, narrow knowledge, or absolute thinking complain that any deviation into the grey is out-of-bounds or "unfair."

Learning to feel comfortable dealing with shades of grey will enhance your *winning at working* results. Often, it's a precursor for consideration to a supervisory or management position. I contend it's a primary reason otherwise talented individuals who want to move ahead, hold themselves back. But even if a management role is not your aspiration, developing the skill of thoughtful, common-sense, situational reflection will serve your work. Before addressing suggestions on how, with tips to enhance shades of grey decision-making, I have three cautionary notes:

1. **Not Everything**
   Not everything should be viewed through shades of grey lenses. Sometimes there's one answer to who you are, and it involves your ethics or integrity. This dictates an unmitigated response. Golfers Bobby Jones, in 1925, and Tom Kite, in 1978, lost their respective tournaments, the *U.S. Open* and the *Hall of Fame Classic*, by one stroke, after rendering self-imposed penalties for something only they knew happened. Both reacted similarly when asked why they did what they did, commenting, "There's only one way to play the game." Sometimes that's true at work, too.

2. **Watch for Suction**
   It's possible to be pulled into darker shades of grey when issues escalate. Instead of admitting an error, acknowledging a mistake, or rethinking the direction, what started as a reasonable decision pulls the decision maker into tenuous circumstances, whirling him down the proverbial "slippery slope." Indicators that you're on this path include small mistruths turning into lies, cover-ups, and irreparable errors. It happened, unknown to us, as a customer. A representative made an unauthorized decision to replace a defective generator at our wilderness cabin. Many mistruths, mishaps, and months later, his decision was uncovered during its installation, nearly costing him his job.

3. **Balancing Act**
   As the complexity of work responsibilities escalate with competing stakeholder interests and outcomes, overlaid with personal principles and

company parameters, it's a balancing act. Sometimes balancing is between compassionate heart and rational head, short-term gains and long-term growth, personal integrity and boss direction, or personal win and bigger winning. But whatever is facing you, look inward. As Fyodor Dostoyevsky put it, "It is not the brains that matter most, but that which guides them—the character, the heart, the generous qualities, progressive ideas."

As I struggled with tendencies of judgmental absolute thinking, I found three concepts enhanced my perspective and increased my ability to operate comfortably in business world shades of grey. Perhaps you'll find these concepts useful as well:

* ★ Understanding Intention
* ★ Seeing the World
* ★ Uncontrollable Expectations

UNDERSTANDING INTENTION

I'm judged by how I look, what I write, what I wear, what I eat, what I read, how I act, how I vote, where I live, who I know or don't know, and a thousand other dimensions. Yet it seems unfair that others might conclude I'm aloof when I'm only shy, distant when I'm overwhelmed, or rude when I'm frightened. It seems equally biased that I might extrapolate from surface elements like someone's appearance, out of control kids, or non-observant behavior to make determinations about them. But I have.

Sometimes I've been quick to evaluate, to smugly assess behavior, and to pass judgment. Those are the times I'd be wise to consider the words of novelist Arnold Bennett, "It is well, when judging a friend, to remember that he is judging you with the same godlike and superior impartiality."

If our children are better behaved, our house is more organized, our career more together, or our body more fit, we consider ourselves more successful. We feel better when we notice others' mistakes, idiosyncrasies, and challenges. That's because when we're judging others, we're really judging ourselves.

Midway in my career, I noticed my judgmental thoughts, recognizing I was evaluating, criticizing, and finding fault more often than I was congratulating, appreciating, and embracing strengths. The more judging my behavior, the less compassionate my actions. That's when I learned about intentions.

Intention awareness changed the way I looked at other people's actions, and my own. It changed most grinding, confrontational, adversarial business and personal relationships into more cooperative, accepting, and professional dealings. It changed absolute thinking into reflective consideration of shades of grey. And it provided exceptional personal growth when I honestly considered my own intentions.

What do you have in mind? That's intention. What is your goal or purpose? That's intention. What do you want as an outcome? To accomplish? That's intention. What is causing you to act the way you're acting? That's intention.

But our intentions are not always what we profess them to be, or think they are. I may think my intention in a spirited debate is to enable the best decision making. But my real intention may be to win the debate, or be perceived as right.

Early in my career, my intention was to be promoted, and I used win strategies to accomplish it. Later, I purposefully changed my intention to making a difference and using my gifts and talents in my work. My approach changed from win to winning because my intention changed. Results and relationships changed as well.

Intentions may be schemes or dreams, wishes or cravings, plans or strategies. They're clues to personal motivation and goal attainment, alerting you to the "why" behind your actions, and whether you're operating with a win or a winning philosophy. Intentions are behavior drivers. Acknowledging yours can change your actions.

Consider the examples below as a mirror. You may discover you're operating with multiple intentions, but select the one central to your action, in the moment. When faced with a difficult or confusing work situation, ask yourself, "What is my intention here? Why am I doing this?"

REFLECTIVE THINKING EXERCISE:
WHAT IS YOUR INTENTION?

Consider the following:

1. When you're engaged in a heated discussion, is your intention to . . .
   • come up with the best solution possible, or demonstrate you're smart?
   • come up with the best solution possible, or win the argument?
   • come up with the best solution possible, or prove your boss wrong?
   • come up with the best solution possible, or win a favorable outcome for yourself or department?
2. When you're working late on a project, is your intention to . . .
   • get the work done as quickly as possible, or get bonus points for staying late?
   • get the work done as quickly as possible, or escape home responsibilities?
   • get the work done as quickly as possible, or continue a woe-is-me story?
   • get the work done as quickly as possible, or build a reputation for delivering?
3. When you go around a co-worker to your boss, is your intention to . . .
   • involve your boss to resolve a critical work issue, or discredit your co-worker?
   • involve your boss to resolve a critical work issue, or get an in with your boss?
   • involve your boss to resolve a critical work issue, or help a client or customer?
   • involve your boss to resolve a critical work issue, or score political currency?

(continued on p. 180)

(continued from p. 179)

4. When you're about to hire someone, is your intention to . . .
   - hire the best person for the job, or reduce departmental competition?
   - hire the best person for the job, or find someone comfortable to work with?
   - hire the best person for the job, or find someone who thinks like you?
   - hire the best person for the job, or give your boss what he's asking for?

5. When you pitch a new idea, is your intention to . . .
   - add efficiencies or profits, or develop a new project for yourself?
   - add efficiencies or profits, or help your creativity thrive?
   - add efficiencies or profits, or demonstrate your initiative?
   - add efficiencies or profits, or beat an internal competitor?

Seated in the boardroom, embroiled in a heated discussion with a declared adversary, the ping-pong of seasoned debaters was watched by those present. No one joined our discussion. No one offered assistance or input. No one moved when previously tempered words turned battle ready. Then, the words he spoke made me pause. I realized we had the same intentions. Both of us wanted what was best for company employees. Our disagreement was over method, not purpose.

Once we realized our intentions were aligned, our discussion changed. In time, our relationship did, too. While we rarely supported each others' recommendations, we were more likely to consider them. Personal respect grew.

If you can meet at an intersection of shared intentions, workplace conflicts, disagreements, and misunderstandings are reduced. If you can't, I use the "most-people perspective" rule—most people are doing the best they can with the skills they have at the time. Most people are well-intentioned. Most people are doing what they believe is the right thing to do.

The more you understand the intentions of co-workers, bosses, and staff, without making assumptions about them, the more you'll evolve good working relationships, common ground, and enhanced work results. Here are three behavior cues I find useful when thinking about my own and others' intentions:

Tips for Intention Identification

★ **Attachment-level**
How attached someone is to a particular outcome is an indicator of intention. The more attached the higher the connection. So if your intention is to win the argument, you'll dig in, reject problem solving, reasonable alternatives, and compromises. If your intent is to develop the best idea, you'll be open to different outcomes, brainstorming, input, and critique.

★ **Discomfort-level**
If someone's intention is dishonorable, without ethics or integrity, or she desires to manipulate, trick, or deceive you into making a decision, doing what she wants you to do, or sabotaging your endeavors, there will be a level of discomfort between you. That's not to imply that everyone you're uncomfortable around has ill intentions, but your intuitive gauge will alert and nudge you into awareness—trust yours.

★ **Assumption-level**
There is a presumption of innocence when charged with a crime. The same presumption should apply in everyday workplace occurrences. The assumptions we make about other's motives or intentions can cause us to jump to conclusions, react inappropriately, and escalate conflict. Most people have well-meaning intentions and that's a good first assumption to make.

Understanding intention necessitates a mention of its power to change lives, make a difference, and create life dreams. Here are two examples:

Greater Good

Doris Kearns Goodwin, author of best-selling *Team of Rivals: The Political Genius of Abraham Lincoln,* tells this story illustrating intention as greater good. In 1855, Lincoln was poised to become the senator from Illinois representing the antislavery coalition. It was his personal desire to win the seat. But when the vote stalled after nine ballots, still four votes from the required fifty-one needed by the Whigs to elect Lincoln, he asked to be dropped as a candidate, convincing party members to give their forty-seven votes to Congressman Lyman Trumbull.

Despite party resistance to his request, it was Lincoln's overriding intention that an antislavery senator be elected. Hence, he voluntarily gave up his own aspirations as messenger, for the greater good of the message.

Greater good intention touches hearts: sacrifices parents make for their children, heroism on sidewalks and battlefields, organ donations, first-responders, volunteers, and charitable contributions, to name a few. Yet greater good intentions also fill day-to-day decision making with compromises, idea sharing, collaboration, trust, communication, and passions larger than paychecks and corner offices. Often they're the silent decisions no one but the decider knows about.

Driving Force

Intention drives action. This force powerfully affects lives, helping to create, shape, and manifest dreams. The intention to move to Montana was that for me. That intention started as a dream.

The seed was planted years ago when my husband and I fell in love, talking of someday living in a cabin in the mountains. The cabin dream became a symbol about what mattered to us—about spending more time together, about family and friends, about nurturing our love and awakening our spirits, about intangibles that called to our hearts when tangibles clogged our heads. It represented the future we wanted to create together.

So nestled among the presents each year for twenty-five Christmases, there was always a tribute to our cabin dream. Sometimes handmade, sometimes store-bought, the cabin gift marked our commitment to that vision, as each year we refined the dream.

We added dream parameters: the location in northwestern Montana, moving by the time we turned fifty, bringing meaningful work with us. We added dream dirt: twenty acres we couldn't quite afford to buy or pass up. We added dream fertilizer: trips to learn the community, financial goals, a finalized design. Along the way, we added dream magic: persistence, determination, and passion.

It took twenty-five years of intention to build our cabin. Not the construction, which took three and a half, but weaving together the life structure to enable us to live and work from this remote Rocky Mountain region. During that time, I learned the difference between dreaming and dream-doing, and the driving power behind intention.

I learned a dream must be nurtured, protected, and grown despite setbacks, struggles, frustrations and naysayers. I learned how difficult it is to move a dream forward when life's challenges diminish time and energy, pulling us like gnats against the status-quo vacuum. I learned a dream happens by intentional choice, not by chance. Unlike wishes that stay wishes, dreams can be molded and developed by taking one tiny intentional step, then another and another, and added to or modified without losing the dream's core.

But mostly, I learned it's not the dream that matters, but its pursuit. The choices I made in my career were influenced by my intention to live and work from the mountains of Montana before I turned fifty. It was that intentional dream-doing that built the life I have now. Of course, now my intention is set on new dreams.

What is the driving intention behind your life? What are you trying to manifest in your dreams? Is your intention to find happiness, wealth, fame, success? To make a difference? To solve the energy problem? To raise loving, compassionate children? To run your own company? To write a best-selling book? If you define what you want from life by being clear about your intentions, you can tap into the power of the universe to create it. Some call it the law of attraction; some the power of intention; some "the secret." But whatever you call it, energy and power comes from an intentional approach to creating the life you want.

SEEING THE WORLD

When you're looking for a new car, you see cars. When you're buying a house, you notice houses. When you're pregnant, you see pregnant women, strollers, and babies everywhere. How you orient to the work world, will determine what you see there.

If you believe people are inherently untrustworthy, you'll find untrustworthy people. If you focus on new ideas, you'll glean unusual seeds others miss. And if you think opportunity is plentiful or women are disadvantaged at work, you'll find plenty of examples to back you up either way. What you focus on, changes what you see.

Consider this *Associated Press* headline: "Sex, Shopping and Gambling All in a Day's Work," generated by an interior department report, citing compelling numbers from an investigation that discovered one million log entries involving seventy-seven hundred employees visiting auction, gaming, gambling, and sex sites on company time. The article finished with plans to curb offenses and punish violators.

Employees whose behavior is the equivalent of stealing time, misusing company equipment, and breaking trust with untrustworthy or unprofessional behaviors should face serious repercussions for their choices—don't get me wrong.

But this headline only confirms the belief of some executives that employees can't be trusted. Once, I worked for a company that viewed Internet access as an acceptable risk only for employees with certain titles. As if title alone equals trustworthy behavior. Publicized greed and misdeeds of corporate executives annihilate that theory. Yet if that's how you see the work world, your belief-blinder doesn't allow you to see the shades of grey.

Past the headlines, the article noted these abuses occurred in a department where 80,000 employees have Internet access. Do the math. That means over 72,000 employees are using their access responsibly. For over 90 percent of employees, those behaviors were not "all in a day's work." It seems to me, it's not the rules that need changing here; it's 10 percent of the people.

Unfortunately, there are people who view company time as personal time, thinking anything goes as long as they don't get caught. They don't think policies and regulations apply to them. They look to do the minimum. So if management thinks most employees are like this, that's what they'll find in their world orientation.

I've met thousands of hardworking, trustworthy, dedicated employees who produced exceptional results, brought work home, held themselves to high standards, and took their work and the work relationship seriously. That's my world orientation. To me it's backwards to write rules, limit sound practices, and make short-term decisions with long-term business impact around a delinquent few. If you can't trust the people you work with, find different people. If you can't trust the people you work for, change departments or companies.

If you work for a company that sees the 10 percent as the 90 you'll find restrictive policies, right-or-wrong thinking, reduced flexibility, and decision making in a tightly controlled environment. There's no way to be *hitting your stride* in a culture like that. Find a workplace that sees the 90 percent of trustworthy, hardworking, dedicated employees, and you'll increase your probability of *winning at working*.

Only when you start to identify your filters, blinders, limiting beliefs, narrow focus, and perspectives affecting how you see the world will your thinking evolve to the insightful level noted by Eleanor Roosevelt at the beginning of this chapter.

The world we see incorporates our beliefs, values, experiences, and focus. A powerful change emerges when you recognize, as seventeenth-century author Robert Bolton put it, "A belief is not merely an idea that the mind possesses; it is an idea that possesses the mind."

UNCONTROLLABLE EXPECTATIONS

Yellow, pink, white, and tangerine hibiscus lined the sloped path to our room, interspersed with orchids and ferns framing the cobalt ocean sparkling under the sun's direction. Agreeing to an upgrade charge at check-in to replace a partial ocean-view room with a full view, we were eager to unpack, put on Hawaii appropriate clothes, and launch our vacation.

My anticipation built as we passed koi-filled ponds, admiring the open-style architecture of the hotel. By the time our key unlocked the double doors, my expectations were soaring. My husband didn't need thirty years of marriage to recognize my disappointment. It was neither the room nor the view I'd pictured. Somewhere between check-in and room arrival, my expectations took over, turning a pleasant experience into a not-so-pleasant one.

Yet if I had approached discovering our new view room like unwrapping a birthday present, full of the joy and excitement of surprise and intrigue with no expectations, I would have seen what was there, not what there wasn't. But because I had created my own mind-picture, I missed the charm it held. It took me until the next morning to see that our ground floor room, steps away from a small beach, was lovely, with an intimate terrace for sunset viewing and whale watching.

Funny how even positive expectations or visualized anticipation can get in our way. It did when visits to our under-construction home had me noticing what hadn't been completed, was crafted differently than I thought it would be, or wasn't working as anticipated. Instead of fun visits filled with delight by what was finished, looking great, or turning out better than expected, I frequently left disheartened. It took months after we moved in for me to see and enjoy the house for what it was. Viewing it through the eyes of friends and family helped me relinquish the expectations I was holding onto like a permanent barnacle labeled "supposed-to-be."

Creating expectations we can't control sets up workplace frustration and disappointment. Much of our despair is self-created by what Dr. Fred Luskin, in *Forgive for Good*, describes as an "unenforceable rule." This is "an expectation you have that you do not have the power to make happen."

So when I created an expectation that only if I received a 15 percent increase when I got promoted would I be satisfied, the 12 percent I got disappointed me. Not having the ability to control my boss's decision didn't stop me from setting up an unenforceable rule. Instead of seeing the happy staffer he expected, he encountered a less than enthusiastic one.

What uncontrollable expectations or unenforceable rules have you created at work? According to Dr. Luskin, "The more unenforceable rules you have, the greater likelihood that you will feel agitated and disappointed. The stronger you try to enforce something you cannot control, the worse you will feel."

We create rules about the way our co-workers should behave, our bosses should operate, and our clients should respond. Yet we can't control our co-workers or influence a non-receptive boss or client. And like my trip to Hawaii, we end up disappointed.

These uncontrollable expectations are the functional equivalent of all-or-nothing, absolute thinking. Immoveable positions, like a mouse in a sticky trap, are hazardous to your work well-being, and this-happens-or-I'll-quit scenarios hurt you. Shifting awareness to hoping something works out moves you directionally into shades of grey.

What you control is different from what you might be able to influence. But you can only influence someone if they allow themselves to be influenced, and some issues you can't influence at all.

REFLECTIVE EXERCISE: WHAT CAN I CONTROL?

Circle the statements below that you control:

1. Your performance
2. Your performance rating
3. The salary you accept when hired
4. The salary increase you receive
5. Your teenager's curfew
6. The time your teenager comes home
7. What your staff thinks of you
8. How you treat your staff
9. If you trust your boss
10. If your boss trusts you
11. Whether you ask for what you need in your budget
12. Whether your budget gets approved
13. If your top employee resigns
14. If your top employee knows she's valued
15. Your child's spelling test score
16. Time helping your child study for her spelling test

Self-Assessment Scoring
You can control 1, 3, 5, 8, 9, 11, 14, and 16. You may be able to influence others, but stop yourself from making them unenforceable rules.

Sometimes our expectations help us. They become self-fulfilling prophecies that enable us to look forward, visualize, and achieve. Sometimes they don't. They can block our view and get in our way by creating a disparity between what was imagined and what is. In these cases, expectations operate like a myopic lens focusing us on what isn't, not what is. When that happens, we miss seeing what's here, right now. We miss out on opportunities, new ventures, and personal development.

There are times for expectations and times for relinquishing them. Expectations make limited sense when you can't control their outcome.

WHEN SHADES TURN MUDDY

Some people get lost in the grey where every issue is full of muddy nuances, subtleties, and possible outcomes. Maybe they're afraid to make a decision; maybe they're lazy; maybe they're overwhelmed; maybe they're incompetent; maybe they can't decide. Whatever the reason, they operate with too many maybes in the land of wishy-washy. I once had a masterful boss permanently housed at that address.

One day she'd give a "definite maybe," the next an "indefinite perhaps," but most of the time, it was "I'll think about it and get back to you." Of course, she never did and no amount of follow-up produced an answer. I came to realize there was a black hole in her desk where decision requests were held. Usually time ran out on the issue, the opportunity passed, or no-decision was rendered. Her staff felt thwarted and frustrated.

Later, I discovered it was just as frustrating to work with, as to work for, these wishy-washy maybe-people. Intertwined projects, assistance, or information needed from other departments and common company goals mean dependence on others to accomplish our work responsibilities. Having to deal with indecisive maybe-people in a critical role or on a team means stalled progress.

Like the Scottish proverb says, "Maybe's a big book," and it's a book I don't like to read or to use. At least not for long. It's one thing to use think time to make the best decision you can and another to let a decision happen by default because you never got around to making your own.

I learned it's better to hear a quick "no" and move on to other options, projects, or opportunities than wander in the land-of-maybe where little can be accomplished. In many workplaces, "maybe" has become the diplomatic, politically correct way to say "no." So the sooner you decide if that applies to your situation, the sooner you can move to Plan B and get results.

However, the problem with too many maybes is not limited to those we need decisions from. We're all decision makers no matter our role. There are teammates, clients, customers, family, or friends you owe information to, responses to, decisions to. The difference in how you decide will leave its mark. Writer and philosopher Gordon Graham puts it this way, "Decision is a sharp knife that cuts clean and straight; indecision, a dull one that hacks and tears and leaves ragged edges behind it."

Being decisive keeps us from getting lost in the grey. Review. Consider. Decide. You see, "life isn't always black and white," but it isn't always grey either. And when it is grey, there still comes a time for a decision or you won't move forward.

BEYOND THE WORKPLACE

Absolute thinking limits creativity, possibility, and opportunity. It reduces discovery, learning, and personal development. It blocks options and shelves imagination. In the words of critic Brooks Atkinson, "The most fatal illusion is the settled point of view. Since life is growth and motion, a fixed point of view kills anybody who has one."

When we reinforce our beliefs only with aligned thinking, we stagnate. When we operate with a my-way-or-the-highway orientation, we eliminate exploration and new pathways. And when we see life as *always* black and white, we limit who we are capable of becoming and never hit our stride.

10

WAKING UP

"The world is full of temptations—they're the wrong things that seem right at the time."
Jiminy Cricket, *Pinocchio*

It's not as if an alarm clock woke me one morning, jarring me to a new perspective, enlightening me to my life's errors, and welcoming me to a new life. I'm a deep sleeper, and it was no different about my work.

"I don't know what you do for a living," Dr. Miller, the emergency room physician, told me as he signed my admission papers. "But whatever it is, I'd consider doing something else. Your body can't take much more of this." Pneumonia, flu, strep throat, and anemia logged on my chart as I entered what became a ten-day hospital stay.

This shouldn't have surprised me. Months earlier, a loving husband, caring family, devoted staff, and insightful friends cautioned me to slow down. Ignoring them, I proudly displayed my superwoman name tag as I blocked internal whispers reminding me to take care of myself. When the whispers became a roar, I promptly stomped out the inner voice warning that a daily four-hour commute, plus a demanding job and family obligations, were exacting a price.

When people said I was driven, I took it as a compliment. Taking care of myself didn't make my priority list. Proving myself, honoring my word, and completing a project on time did make the list, like most everyone and everything else in my life. I was selfless, I thought, adding mental points to my scorecard, as I blindly ignored an emerging trend.

At the time, I told my hospital story like a badge of courage, thinking it illustrated my strong work ethic. Today, I know, it illustrates my foolishness. Then, I believed my internal press releases, thinking the work I was doing was more important. I'm not sure what I was thinking? More important than living my life? More important than following my dreams? More important than the people I love?

A year after my emergency room encounter, I changed jobs, which led to deeper wake-up nudges years later when I experienced the seductive side of power, influence, and money. But the theme of this chapter is not my personal difficulty hearing repetitive wake-up calls or peeling the faux layers of my onion. This chapter is about recognizing nudges, identifying choices for your life, and seeing the opportunities you can create as you invent your future. It's about finding what matters to you.

What I learned from several companies, jobs, positions, relationships, stumbles, and achievements is this—as you build your life, your life builds you. Sometimes that building takes you in a direction that nourishes your soul and ignites your uniqueness, and sometimes it doesn't. When it does, you feel alive, vibrant, self-confident, motivated, enthusiastic, and engaged. You're connected to your life and moving in the direction of your aspirations and dreams.

But when building your life takes you away from the core of who you are, causing you to lose the authentic self-connection, even for a little while, you'll unearth inklings about the path you're on. These come in multiple flavors: stress, frustration, anger, resentment, fear, and irritation, to name a few. Of course, you may hide them from yourself. I did, believing the life I was building with bigger titles, more responsibility, and an accumulation of financial trappings was the one I sought.

Occasionally, when I stopped long enough to notice, I caught myself looking at the person in the mirror whose face I knew, but who was disconnected from me. She looked familiar, but the essence behind her eyes was blurry and vague. These were the times I avoided in-depth self-reflection, busying myself with more to-dos, believing they were things that mattered.

I was living the reality of author Gary Zukav's words, "Your emotions tell you what your soul wants you to know." Something gnawed below the surface impressions of my success, confidence, and well-being. For years, I ignored the gnawing, hints, and clues until, like a dormant volcano, my unexpected explosions dispersed verbal steam on unsuspecting loved ones, staff, or colleagues, leaving me wondering who was this person I had become?

REFLECTIVE EXERCISE: IS SOMETHING GNAWING YOU?

On a scale of 1 to 5, rate how often the following statements are true for you.

1 (Rarely) 2 (Not Often) 3 (Sometimes)
4 (Frequently) 5 (More Often than Not)

1. I complain about my boss, co-workers, or the work I do.
2. I think about changing jobs.
3. I feel angry, whether I display outward signs or not.
4. I dread going to work, especially on Mondays.
5. I wonder if I'm missing out; "Isn't there more to life?"
6. I'm drained, exhausted or unmotivated.
7. I feel I have to hide who I am or compromise my passions to fit in.
8. I take my work frustrations out on my friends, partner, or children.
9. I numb work stress with food, alcohol, drugs, or other unhealthy or addictive behaviors.
10. I have trouble going or staying asleep.
11. I feel the treadmill I'm on speeding up and can't see a way to get off.
12. No one hears me or "gets" who I am.
13. There's no time for me on my priority list.
14. I delay taking a vacation, and then when I do, I end up working part of it. (*continued on p. 194*)

(*continued from p. 193*)

15. I haven't achieved what I want or followed my dreams because of other people's influence or lack of support.
16. My life is living me more than I'm living my life.
17. I'm not comfortable without busyness or connections around me: e-mail, texting, cell phone, PDA.
18. I miss family events or children's activities because of work.
19. I experience road-rage, shop-rage, or other forms of life-rage.
20. I'm looking for the next adrenaline high, next promotion, next big project, next salary hike, next . . . next . . . next.

Self-Assessment Scoring

If you scored *less* than 55, more likely than not, you're using your gifts and helping invent the future you want. If you scored *more* than 55, something could be gnawing at you. A visit or re-visit to the reflective exercises in Chapter Seven, "Bringing Yourself to Work," may kindle self-knowledge.

A JOB IS NOT A JOB

It only happened on Mondays. Sometimes I escaped the unpleasant ritual. But more often than not, right before boarding, I threw up in the ladies room of the train station. It wasn't the commute I hated. It was the job.

The reasons don't matter why a job I once enjoyed turned into a job I didn't. It happens. Bosses change, companies change, priorities change, budgets change, responsibilities change. Some changes bring personal growth and opportunity. Some don't.

What does matter is this lesson that stayed with me—a job is not just a job. It affects your health, well-being, relationships, and life. While that job I hated helped my checking account, my confidence, creativity, health, energy for life, and view of the world were not as fortunate.

When the alarm clock rang, my previous excitement to face a new day became cocoon-like behavior, both in and out of the covers, seeking protection from another day's battle. It was safer for those I loved to refrain from sharing important issues with me, never knowing how I'd react.

How you spend a significant part of your day rubs off on the rest of your day, and on those you share your life with. Over time, it rubs off on your life, too. I'm not talking about temporary potholes and work hiccups that come with change, periods of work intensity, interim choices to increase finances, or normal setbacks and challenges that should be dealt with at work. I'm talking about the long-term match between who you are and the job you have.

When you're in a job that's good for you, when you're *hitting your stride*, you can feel it, and you can feel it when you're not. I agree with author and personal growth expert Barbara de Angelis, "No job is a good job if it isn't good for you." You can't be *winning at working* if you don't like what you're doing, where you're doing it, or whom you're doing it for or with.

If what you do feels like work the majority of the time, consider why and what you can do to change it. That doesn't necessarily mean changing jobs or companies. Transferring to another team, volunteering for a new project, or asking your boss for new responsibilities may be all it takes. But whatever it takes, you won't be able to offer your best you at work and get rewarded with interesting work, personal growth, and financial rewards, if you aren't in a good workplace environment and in a position that matches who you are, what you want, and what you have to offer.

I've worked in jobs where I couldn't wait until Monday. I've been fortunate that way the majority of my career. That's when I'm so excited about the project, idea, or the next thing I'm working on that it's not work to me. It's a challenging, interesting, stimulating, and fun way to spend my day. I'm a lot happier when that's the case. So are my family and friends.

REFLECTIVE EXERCISE: MY WORK HAPPINESS FACTOR

Personal insight is more likely if you write your answers.

1. Thinking about the jobs I've had, when was the last time
(*continued on p. 196*)

(*continued from p. 195*)

I was excited about going to work? Why? Describe the work, boss, and environment. How is that the same or different from right now?

2. If I worked for myself, I'd be engaged in what type of work activities? List five to ten. Rank them. How does that compare with now?

3. I am excited and challenged when I do what kind of tasks? What work am I doing when I'm the most motivated?

4. List the responsibilities you enjoy in your job. Now the ones you don't. How balanced is the list? What can you do to create more of those you enjoy, while still meeting your job responsibilities?

5. When my work feels like work, it's because of the following factors: list them. Next to each one, imagine you're a coach, coaching you. Offer one suggestion to improve your work experience.

6. If I won the lottery tomorrow, I would stay in my job or leave my job? Why or why not?

7. If I could take a work do-over, knowing what I know now about the work I do, I would make the following changes? What's stopping me from making those changes anyway?

8. I would define "work" as? I would define "my work" as? I would define my "work passion" as?

9. If I were to share a dream about my life with someone I trusted, I'd tell him about my long-held desire to do what?

10. Looking back on my worklife in ten, fifteen, or twenty years, the biggest regret if I stay on this path is? What can I do now to make sure that is not a regret I encounter?

LOOKING FOR SOMETHING

Taped to the locked door of the deserted ranger station, the handwritten message with yesterday's date noted that the lava was flowing three miles away. Look for a lone tree on the western slope of the foothills, it guided. That's all the information we had as we set out across the immense lava field on the Big Island of Hawaii, searching for the breakout and knowing where it was yesterday might not be where it was today.

For three hours we hiked toward the foothills, every step

carefully planted to traverse the uneven, jagged black-brown old lava, at times like hurled pillars blocking our way. With no map to guide us, no trail to follow, and no feedback to know if the way we were heading was right, it was a difficult and confusing journey.

We found the lava flow unexpectedly. We weren't clear how it would look, so fortunately the air alerted me to the danger, not the slick, silvery cooling lava in front of me. Only because I was having trouble breathing did I stop. Then I noticed the red glow in the blackened rocks, no more than twenty feet ahead.

Sometimes my life is like that hike. I'm searching for something I'm eager to find. It's not that I'm lost exactly, but I'm confused how I will know it, which way to go, and where the directions are. Since there's no clear path, it's as if I'm wandering through life searching for something I can't quite articulate.

Occasionally I locate what becomes, for me, a seductive splinter trail, like the achievement path I followed for a time, believing if I proved myself, got ahead, or became successful I'd find what I was looking for. But I didn't.

I've searched the new-experience path, the accumulation-of-stuff path, the other-people-can-make-me-happy path, the learning-path, the follower-leader path, the when-this-happens-I'll-be-fulfilled path, and numerous others. While all those journeys have shaped and evolved my life, they left me feeling a bit empty, yearning for something.

What I woke up to realize is it wasn't out there, because I was really looking for me. Not "looking for" as in lost, but rather hidden from view. I'd been on life's journey from the outside in, not the inside out. I'd been looking to discover my gifts, talents, passions, purpose, meaning, or individual path out there.

Instead, I've come to understand, in the words of mountain climber and explorer Edmund Hillary, "It's not the mountain we conquer, but ourselves." Like the lava we found that day in Hawaii, eking its way to the surface from the earth's core, who we are flows from our center. The only way to find that is to follow the path within.

I don't suggest this excursion as an exclusive path or a

me-centered approach, but as a parallel, integrated-into-the-world one. While an idyllic, inner-wisdom, meditative avenue may tempt you to retreat, the world needs people who authentically show up and offer their soulful, best of self-presence in everyday, ordinary ways. One caution: don't expect an inner awareness journey to be straight, fast, or clear. Insights at one age may seem short-sighted at another. My experience (so far) involves vistas, backtracking, detours, holding patterns, difficult hills, hidden valleys, and wonderful surprises.

WANTING WHAT YOU WANT

Pouring myself a bowl of soup from the buffet line, I noticed a teenage boy standing slightly behind a grandmotherly woman eyeing the last piece of chocolate cake. After a contemplative pause, she reached for apple cobbler, and the teenager swooped in on his prize. Turned out they didn't want the same dessert after all.

Watching them piqued my curiosity. I started noticing each diner emerging from the buffet line, eyeing their tray for choices. There were occasional similarities, but no two were identical. While my casual observations were far from scientific, they did get me thinking.

Often we believe we want the same things from life as other people, but we don't. We conjecture that everyone wants what we do and live our lives in competition, trying to achieve, acquire, or get what we think everyone is after. We search for meaning, purpose, or connection because we think we're supposed to find it, versus make it. Or we imagine others know something we don't, so we follow their definitions and their desires.

We're influenced by advertising, celebrity stories, and media hype, each transforming those messages into desires or needs we never knew we had. We confuse our wants with those others have for us, or ones we believe we're supposed to have. And we put pressure on others, unknowingly, as we assume spouses, family, and friends should want what we do, imposing our thoughts, wants, wishes, and needs on them.

But life is like that buffet table. We want different things. Our tastes, interests, gifts, and circumstances influence our dreams and desires. But many of us haven't defined what they are. We don't know what we want out of our life, so how can we draw into it what we desire? How can we create the life we seek to live?

It took me decades to uncover that what I thought I wanted, I didn't; what I believed successful people were supposed to want was empty, for me, once I got there. The expected high was absent. Still, I searched. It must be over the next mountain, in the next goal attainment, or down the next path. I didn't know exactly what "it" was, but I kept looking to the outside.

I've learned I can decide much of my life. It's as individual as my buffet preferences. To do that, I need to define what I want, believe I can have it, and visualize and evolve it into existence. We help create the world we want. My life shouldn't be filled with what others think it should be. It shouldn't be filled with someone else's measurements for success or achievement or happiness. That yardstick is mine.

Someone else's wants can't bring you happiness, contentment, or delight even if you get them. For that kind of joy, you need to "hear" and act on the desires of your heart. I remember telling someone of my dream to live in the mountains of Montana. His reaction was not expected. "I can't imagine wanting something like that," he said. "Why in the world would you want to live out in the middle of nowhere?" But for me, it wasn't nowhere, it was a magical and evocative place.

What about you? What do you want? Picture it. Dream it. Desire it. Believe you can have it. Then take one tiny action step in that direction. Now, do it again. Picture it. Dream it. Believe you can have it. Take another action step. Even if those steps are months or years apart, keep moving in the direction of your dreams. Keep inventing the future you desire.

FINDING WHAT MATTERS

I was born in Montana. Leaving at three, I was raised in

southern California, college educated in northern California, graduate-school educated in Michigan, and career focused in Pennsylvania. Along the way of growing up, falling in love, raising a family, and having a career, Montana was part of my life in one way or another, calling me back to hike the trails in Glacier National Park, snowshoe on Big Mountain, and build a cabin on the North Fork of the Flathead River. Each time I went, it was harder to leave.

Over the years, the dream of living in Montana became a driving force in my life. So did my career. Climbing the corporate ladder to vice president for QVC, I thrived on the challenge, the excitement, and the creativity of my work. I managed hundreds of people and millions of dollars. Yet behind the achievements, the nice paychecks, and the challenging work, something was missing. Of course, I couldn't see it then. But, when I was honest with myself, I could feel it.

Seduced by what I was doing, I lost sight of why I was doing it. My life was very full: full of meetings, answering e-mails, listening to voice mails, and initiating and completing projects. The people I cared about most became one more task on my to-do list, one more interruption to a pressing deadline.

Along the way, I managed to lose my way. I got so caught up in the things that didn't matter, that I couldn't always see the things that did. Even my wonderful marriage began to show signs of stress, as my angry outbursts became a frequent visitor, and extra-strength Excedrin was added as a staple to my diet.

Montana continued to call my name, louder. I noticed it more. I talked about it more, sharing with bosses and staff my long-held dream. It kept me focused year after year, work challenge after work challenge, to know the stepping stones to transitioning to this new life were gradually being laid.

I wish I could tell you it was easy leaving a life lived for twenty-something years, transporting myself to idyllic surroundings, and turning on the dream-magic. But it didn't happen that way. Enticed by power, influence, money, status, and ego-trappings, I had a difficult time discerning the real-me, from the person I'd morphed to fill. As we came closer to moving to Montana, my resistance took hold, and then my fear.

I felt lost as I clung to the job and life I had, even taking on new responsibilities and pitching new projects, as I grasped for the familiar. "How can I leave what I'm doing?" I asked my husband. Of course, what I meant was, "How can I leave *who* I am?" Without my job, I feared I'd have no identity, no sense of self. When who I am is not what I do, then who am I?

Realizing who you are pretending to be is not who you are, challenges at a core level. But you can't hold new possibilities with clenched fists or view new opportunities with closed eyes. So when the terror of losing my identity became less than the pull of my dream, I let go.

In July 2002, my husband, Dan, and I left the suburbs of Philadelphia and moved to Montana. I left my job to pursue a life dream to live and write from the mountains I loved, with a lifestyle I yearned to explore. The nudges in my life had pushed, pulled, and yanked me awake, realizing there are no promised tomorrows, this is not a practice round, and finding what matters is what matters.

Of course, on this safari of life, the discovery of what matters continues to deepen, evolve, broaden, and refine me, as new dreams emerge.

A NEW DEFINITION OF WORK

Some people compartmentalize life. There's work and there's life. I'm in a different camp. To me, your work is a pursuit of your life. Or, in the words of Buddha, "Your work is to discover your work and then with all your heart to give yourself to it." Life is not what happens outside of work, but what's created with the gifts and talents you have and the choices you make. It's not what you can get from life, but what you can give to it.

Who I am today is a reflection of all paths taken and all choices made or not made. For me, waking up is an ongoing process of evolving and growing and becoming. I'm still waking to my life and its potential, still becoming who I am and who I'm not, still learning what I want and don't want, and still discovering life's treasures.

I determined it wasn't what I *was doing* at work that gnawed at me; it was what I *wasn't* doing. Not offering my gifts, not showing up, not following my dreams, not embracing my passions could have been my life's regret. Instead, I woke up and decided it wouldn't be.

What about you?

PART THREE

BEHIND CLOSED DOORS

"The greatest discovery of my generation is that human beings can alter their lives by altering their attitudes of mind."
William James

POSTSCRIPT: FROM A BOSS'S PERSPECTIVE

"Every man takes the limits of his own field of vision for the limits of the world." **Arthur Schopenhauer**

This postscript is comprised of short essays and thoughts. Consider them as individual fly-on-the-wall glimpses into the boss's office, or an opportunity to eavesdrop on thoughts and conversations to discover what a boss might like to say, but often can't or won't, especially on those already stress-filled days.

This chapter is not like other chapters, written to motivate, inspire, or offer tips. Rather, it's a cautionary note with "boss" perspectives not normally communicated. Of course, I'm not suggesting bosses think these thoughts every day or in unison. So consider this a road sign alerting you that sometimes there's "Uneven Pavement Ahead."

Caution: some messages come with an edge. If it feels that way to you, remember my intention is to offer you help to navigate the murky, confusing, boss waters. This postscript is a well-meaning, albeit sometimes pointed, heads-up. Like the Montenegrin proverb puts it, "Advice is like medicine, the better it is, the nastier to take."

CLOSED DOORS

I used to wonder what went on behind closed doors, until I had a door to close. I'm here to tell you, it's not what you think. It surprised me the first time I heard rumors about a meeting I had attended as a recently promoted VP, since the rumors had nothing to do with the meeting content discussed. When the boss closes the office door, it seems rumors kick into high gear.

The eyes glancing from behind cubicle walls note who's with the boss, how long he stays, and of course, the status of open or shut door. The assumption is a closed door equates to something going on, even if no one is with the boss. She must be working on something confidential, right? Not necessarily.

Sure, sometimes that's correct. The door is closed because the topic requires confidentiality. But most times that's not the case. Bombarded with questions, issues, problems, interruptions, and requests, a boss may close the door simply as a stop sign.

Consider that a boss's day is rarely hers. It's brimming with meetings, conference calls, staff queries, problems, and priority changes. Let me dispel any closed-door mysteries by sharing a few reasons mine was shut. It . . .

- ★ gave the other person my uninterrupted attention.
- ★ signaled my assistant and immediate staff I was occupied.
- ★ allowed for an engaging meeting without disturbing people outside.
- ★ let me shoot the breeze with a colleague or vent with someone I trusted.
- ★ provided a quiet sanctuary to do pressing work.
- ★ helped me think, plan, and be strategic.
- ★ offered a place to calm down, contain emotions, or get a "game face" on.
- ★ offered privacy to resolve pressing or upsetting personal or family issues.
- ★ allowed for coaching, counseling, or encouraging staff members.
- ★ created a barrier for others to cool down after difficult conversations.
- ★ stopped outside distractions, conversations, and voice pollution.
- ★ enabled returning a series of phone calls on a variety of topics.

* allowed strong words to be spoken to an outside supplier, vendor, or consultant, while maintaining their confidentiality.
* gave me a break to eat lunch while catching up on e-mail.

Don't waste time trying to figure out what's going on behind your boss's closed door because the answer, more often than not, is nothing out of the ordinary. More importantly, don't get caught up in rumor sparks initiated by others' speculation. Don't worry about what your boss is doing, and while you're at it, don't worry about what the person down the hall is doing, either.

I did close the door when Jeff came to see me for the third time in as many weeks. Once again, sitting across the desk, Jeff was expressing distress. He was upset Lydia was making more money than he was. Last week, he was unhappy with the hours Joe wasn't putting in, leaving at five when he was often stuck past six. The week before, he registered a complaint about the way work assignments were handed out by his supervisor. As my mother would say, "Same song, thirtieth verse."

Jeff's focus was on everything but his work. He fixated on the latest rumors, viewed work policies as unfair, kept track of what was happening down the hall, and fretted over what others might be getting that he wasn't. As a result, his own acres were filled with uncultivated opportunities and backlogged projects.

I've met and managed too many Jeffs; people focused on everyone except themselves. They fritter away time trying to straighten out others. They complain, blame, and point fingers. They believe the world owes them a living, others are out to get them, and nothing goes their way. You can recognize their victim mindset and frequent anthem, "It's not fair."

They're right. Work life isn't fair, but then, what is? Does fair mean equal pay increases and work assignments? What people offer to the workplace isn't equal, so how would that be fair if rewards were? Unbiased? Well, we all have biases, and life happens to be subjective. Is life just? If just means one gets what's merited, then for people like Jeff, the workplace is pretty just. They get back what they give, which is not much. That doesn't mean the issues they raise are not valid at times, but like Chicken Little, frequent complainers are tuned out.

Here's a message to all the Jeffs and rumor igniters out there: pay attention to your five acres, put your energy into your performance, get results, and you'll get rewarded. Stop focusing on everyone else, including your boss. In the words of novelist Aldous Huxley, "There is only one corner of the universe you can be certain of improving, and that's your own self."

THE SANDBOX

I don't want to hear about your argument with Susan, or that you're not getting along with Bob's department, or the latest gossip spreading like honey on a hot day. I don't care why you think Janice did better in budget approvals than you did, or why you feel you've been slighted. And I certainly don't want to hear your victim stories.

Grow up. Bosses are not referees, therapists, or parents. We don't want to be pulled into squabbles or asked to resolve them. You were hired because we thought you were an adult. Get out of your sandbox and handle it. Solve your relationship problems, or do everything you can possibly think of to resolve them before coming to us with your problems.

I expect you to be accountable for your actions. That means, if you don't get the raise, promotion, or more interesting work, or if you have challenging relationships with your co-workers or with me, you'll look in the mirror first.

Many sandbox behaviors are labeled company politics. I'd categorize capers like self-serving antics, sabotaging behaviors, information hoarding, and artful manipulation under this heading. I'd throw in veiled threats, perpetuated mistruths, finger-pointing, and coercion.

But company politics don't have to be a bloody sandbox

sport. Strategic alignments, interdepartmental collaboration, and volunteering for work assignments are politics, too. The politics label can be assigned when assisting other departments, supporting company initiatives, cooperating with those in charge, sharing information, and helping achieve results. That's because politics can be served with a negative or a positive impact.

It's the intention behind your action that determines whether politics creates fear or builds relationships, whether it's sandbox behavior or career-enhancing activity. What's your motive? If politics is a dirty word where you work, undermining results and reducing engagement, consider your contribution to that culture.

You have a choice how you use your power and influence, and don't be naive to think you don't have both. You can serve your brand of politics from well-intentioned thoughts or manipulative self-interest, and each has a different impact. How you serve your politics at work is a direct result of how you show up, in the deepest sense, as a person. But to do that, you have to leave the sandbox behind.

WHY THE ANSWER IS ALWAYS "NO"

It's easier to say "yes." It's easier to have you like me. It's easier to tell you your work is fine. But easier isn't better— not for you and not for me. That's why the answer is "no."

I can't trust you'll deliver your half-baked ideas. Your performance is inconsistent, mediocre, and half-engaged. When you say you'll "handle it," sometimes you do and sometimes you don't. Don't ask for a raise, a promotion, or more interesting assignments. The answer is "no."

Standing outside my office door, I could tell by Jodie's downward glance, she was not there to give me good news on the project. Despite her confident, enthusiastic, and definitive style, she failed to deliver what she had pitched. It was not the first time.

Jodie operated counter to the Scottish proverb advising: "Never let your feet run faster than your shoes." She was full of ideas, full of promise, full of idealism, and short on results. Her over-promising stalled her career. She talked with absolute confidence about what she was going to do, but she didn't do it.

Don't follow in Jodie's footsteps. Don't be like a small-town billboard claiming "best hamburger in the world," or like those books and magazines touting you can have flat abs in five minutes a day, build self-esteem in ten days, or become a millionaire in five easy steps. While promises may be the essence of advertising, and over-promising may get books, magazines, products, and services sold, they cause disappointment. Your unfilled promises will build my hopes, but diminish my trust. So kill the hype.

If you want me to say "yes," take note. There's one approach that defines people who are *winning at working*. They don't disappoint—they deliver. They consistently produce what they say they will. They do it again and again and again. They may pitch their ideas with passion and exuberance, or caution and logic, but they don't hype them.

If anything, they under-promise and over-deliver, without sandbagging. Every time they do what they say they're going to do, they build their credibility, and credibility builds careers. But there's another benefit. Self-esteem soars when you surprise and delight a boss, a client, or a teammate by delivering more than you promised. When you build your knowledge, deliver your work promises, and get performance results consistently, then you'll hear "yes" again and again and again.

HELP ME HELP YOU

If you'd alerted me that you were running into problems or realized you couldn't get the work done, you could have asked for help. It's not weakness, but strength, to admit there's a problem. A heads-up would have enabled me to remove obstacles, negotiate delivery, or shift resources. Remember, I'm on your side, and as your boss, I want you to succeed.

But what if it's bigger than resources or obstacles? What if you made a big, costly mistake? What then? People make mistakes, they trip up sometimes, and they do, on occasion, speak or act in error. And while there's nothing that says you should be happy when that happens, trying to act like it didn't, covering your mistake, or trying to justify an inaccurate position leads nowhere.

So gather your courage, swallow hard, and explain what happened, what went wrong, or what mistake you made. One of the biggest errors you can make at work is pointing fingers, blaming others, or offering excuses. Own your decisions, choices, and actions. Admit when you're wrong. Fix your mistakes. Then learn from them and move on. These are the signs of confident, accountable, initiative-filled people, and these are the people bosses want on their teams.

Playing it safe isn't. Your mistake will eventually be discovered. As your boss, I'll have more confidence in you and respect for you if you come to me and truthfully tell me what happened. I'll even try to help you fix it if I can. So help me help you.

WHAT I CAN'T TELL YOU

Even if you come to my office, look me in the eye, and ask directly, I can't tell you if the company is contemplating an acquisition, merger, or significant reorganization. I can't provide inklings of new endeavors. I probably can't tell you if he resigned or was fired, how the company settled a lawsuit, or if we engaged an executive recruiter to conduct a search for a new officer. Even if you've heard rumors, I can't confirm them. Most of the time, though, if at all possible, I'll tell you that I can't tell you, or that I'm not able to discuss anything. I know it's hard. It is for both of us.

I'm not trying to deceive you. I'm not trying to hide information or imply that I don't trust you. I just can't tell you. Aside from the regulations of publicly traded companies where premature information sharing can affect stock prices, there are contracts, confidentiality agreements, and legal documents in organizations that can preclude the sharing of such information, not to mention personal ethics and integrity.

So after the merger you heard rumored is announced,

don't assume you were deliberately lied to. Don't bad mouth me or other bosses because we didn't share what we couldn't. It's not that we don't want to answer your questions with forthrightness, but our fiduciary obligations often prohibit it.

Now don't confuse what you just read with management accountability for communicating information that can and should be shared. To perform your responsibilities in a competent manner, to offer the best of who you are to the workplace, and to engage your discretionary efforts and intellectual ideas at work, you need information.

You should expect information to be freely and openly provided by your bosses. You should expect dialogue and a work culture of communication and trust. If these elements are present, you won't need to question what I didn't tell you. You'll respect and understand the stakeholder obligations management needs to balance, and you'll have confidence the information will be shared as soon as it can be.

GETTING STARTED WITH ME, YOUR BOSS

Welcome to the team. I'm passionate about my work and saw a similar passion in you during the hiring process. I've eagerly awaited your arrival. You have everything going for you right now. So to help you get started successfully with me and the team, I put together a few performance hints.

* **Learn first**. It doesn't matter how you used to do it where you worked before, or how you think it should be done or done better, learn our business first. Learn our ways first. Ask questions, observe, study, and take it in. Once you understand how it works here, then I'll be open to hearing your thoughts and ideas.
* **New kid on the block**. Everyone is waiting to see if you fit in. I'm wondering if I made the right decision by hiring you. Give us an early indication that you're the right ego-detached, helpful, considerate, competent, friendly, results-oriented, truthful, and engaged person we desire for our team.

★ **Ask the right person.** Ask me about the department or company vision, goals, or direction. Ask me about expectations and how we work in this department. Ask me what I expect. Ask me about your responsibilities and role, and how I'd like to be communicated with. But ask someone else how to set up your phone or computer or do the nitty-gritty of your job. Be resourceful. Figure it out.

★ **More.** Give me back more than I ask. Surprise and delight me with your work ethic, integrity, and involvement. Volunteer for assignments. Sign up for training. Get engaged.

★ **My work.** Your work is important, but my work is more important. This isn't ego, it's economics. I get paid more than you do for a reason. What I do adds more value to the company than what you do, right now, at this moment. You may far exceed me in your career, but now you don't. Think of your time with me as billable hours. Come prepared to spend the time wisely.

★ **Give me facts.** You may not understand why I'm asking a question or why the information I'm seeking is important, but I need you to answer factually so I can make good decisions. If I don't ask the specific question, volunteer what you know about the topic in question. Silence is not golden on this team.

★ **Favorites.** Yes, I have favorites—people I trust. People who deliver. People who are passionate. These people get the best assignments, raises, and opportunities. But you can become a favorite, too. There's no limit to how many people can be *winning at working* on this team.

★ **Winning, not win.** If you've been a win player, you might find it different operating with winning philosophies and behaviors. This team is an amazing team. Join us fully, or leave us quickly. It's a short honeymoon. More than likely, you have two or three weeks before I assess the decision to add you to the team. While I may not know in two weeks if you'll succeed, I will know if I have doubts. Don't give me any.

BOSSES ARE PEOPLE TOO

Yes, I did overreact this morning, but it wasn't caused by you or your proposal. Yes, my sarcasm was a bit cutting. I had a blow-up with my husband before leaving for the office, so when you caught me first thing, I snapped. I probably should have explained or said I'm sorry, but I didn't. That line between personal and professional is a tightrope, and while I'm not expecting sympathy for a path I chose to follow, I tell you in candor, it's often lonely up here.

I can't share when I'm terrified or when I'm extra stressed because you're depending on me to have answers, clear obstacles, and lead the way. I can't tell you I'm preoccupied that my father was diagnosed with Alzheimer's, my son received a detention, or the stock market precipitated a gut-wrenching margin call, because it might diminish your confidence in my ability. It might even expose me to workplace gossip.

I don't dare express that I didn't sleep again last night because work pressures have taken over my life, or that I'm no longer motivated at work, or I've lost confidence in my boss, because how I feel about work can affect how you feel, and that's not fair to you.

So here's my boss message. The reaction you interpret as having something to do with you probably doesn't. Bosses aren't issued a superman or superwoman cape when promoted. They feel pressure. They make mistakes. And they're not invincible from "life happens" occurrences. Life crashes down on them from time to time, and can affect their work performance, mood, and motivation, too.

But they know the "show must go on" no matter how they're feeling. They're accountable to the dozens or hundreds or thousands of people counting on them. People whose livelihood, mortgages, and families depend on the company being profitable or reaching objectives, so that their jobs can continue.

Bosses put their game face on, act the part, and learn to compartmentalize personal and work priorities. Sometimes at work or behind the scenes, they're not as together or as invincible as you may expect them to be. So here's the bottom-line about bosses . . . don't expect perfect. Expect human.

A FEW CLOSING THOUGHTS

The bosses I've worked for, and the people I've worked with, enabled me to navigate my work with fresh perspective and gained insights. They helped me find my stride. Some relationships were difficult, but each provided growth. May you discover the contributions that the people you work for, and with, can offer you, even in times of conflict, challenge, and frustration. No matter their roles, if you're fortunate, they'll push, stretch, challenge, and spark your development.

Please don't follow advice or tips in this book unless it enhances your work, your way. My way isn't your way. Any advice taken should enhance your gifts and uniqueness, ring true to you, make sense for this time in your life, push you from a confining comfort zone into a blossoming possibility, or embrace your dreams.

I make no claim to being right, nor do I have any illusions of wisdom or importance in writing this book. I've shared ideas, thoughts, suggestions, and insights with you as a gift from one generation to another; as a way to give back what I've been given along my way. Please take and interpret what works for you and leave the rest.

I have much heart in this book. If you found it helpful, I'd love to hear from you. Feel free to write me at info@nanrussell.com or P.O. Box 1327, Whitefish, MT 59937, and let me know which parts, tips, insights, or messages made some difference for you.

But more importantly, if this book was helpful to you, please pass the message along. Give this book to someone you care about at work so they, too, can be *hitting their stride*, because only when we're all winning, will we truly all win.

READER'S RESOURCE TO
HITTING YOUR STRIDE

As you offer the best of who you are to the workplace, uniquely *hitting your stride*, this resource may be a helpful reminder, reference, or *winning at working* summary to aid your journey. To download a PDF copy, go to www.hittingyourstridenow.com.

---

winning at working \ *philosophy.* \ **1.** offering the best of who you are to the workplace, with or without climbing the company hierarchy, and being rewarded with interesting work, personal growth, and financial gain **2.** igniting your gifts and talents by bringing yourself to work or offering your uniqueness to the world through your work **3.** consciously operating with a foundational perspective that when we're all *winning*, we *all* win. **4.** see also www.winningatworking.com

---

hitting your stride \ *verb.* \ **1.** your work, your way. **2.** what it *looks like* for *you* to be *winning at working.* **3.** your pace, your talents, your highest you shining through. **4.** your uniqueness applied with ease and grace.

FOUNDATIONAL PHILOSOPHIES
Core philosophies that encompass winning principles, behaviors, and concepts:

★ How you do what you do matters (with ease, grace, and gratitude).

★ You get what you give (law of reciprocity).
★ The power behind your intentions (law of attraction).
★ Offering the best of who you are (authentic self).
★ Bringing you-ness to the world (your uniqueness).
★ Your work, your way (making your work, work for you).
★ Living your life's potential (why you're here).
★ Creating your future (realizing your dreams).
★ Fueling your passion (embracing your life).
★ A sense of service (making a difference).
★ When we're all winning, we all win (a better world).

TEN *WINNING AT WORKING* WAYS

Concepts and actions that support a *winning at working* philosophy:

1. Creating Your Own Luck
   How real people get ahead—initiative
   Establishing personal brand and performance trust
   Performance differentiation with uncommon practices

   ★ And then some
   ★ Taking your words seriously
   ★ Take it or leave it . . . but get it
   ★ Those little things
   ★ A dose of the Ds
   ★ Your ROI
   ★ Ego-detached
   ★ A bit of Pollyanna

2. Don't Be Blowing in the Wind
   Finding and using your voice
   Quieting your mind when you listen
   Keeping off the path of least resistance
   Having the courage to ask
   Developing the courage to tell
   Finding the courage to leave

Honoring others' gifts
Making a commitment to self
Being about your future, not your past

8. A Practice of Trust
As a door to your spirit
Authentic trust comes from authentic people
Self-trust; can't trust others if don't trust self
Creating your pockets of excellence
Giving trust first
Showing up: WYSIWYG (What You See Is What You Get)
Communication as trust key

9. Shades of Grey
Seeing the grey; enhancing the human-side
Your intention drives your actions
Taking paths for the greater good
Your beliefs determine what you can see
Beware of your uncontrollable expectations

10. Waking Up
A job is not a job
Wanting what you want
Hearing the nudges in your life
Finding what matters to you

WINNING AT WORKING PRINCIPLES

Guiding basics to *hitting your stride*

accountability	doing	resilience
authenticity	dream	respect
commitment	excellence	self-awareness
communication	gratitude	service
courage	honesty	soul-enhancing
credibility	initiative	trust
desire greatness	integrity	
determination	intention	
discipline	passion	

Winning at Working Tips

Reflective Exercises

NOTES AND PERMISSIONS

"Feeling gratitude and not expressing it is like wrapping a present and not giving it." **William Arthur Ward**

OVERALL

Quotations used in this book, unless otherwise cited, were taken from the author's collection of motivational, inspirational, and compelling quotations; collector since 1981.

A special thank you to these authors who enhanced my perspective on various themes and philosophies in this book:

Deepak Chopra, *The Seven Spiritual Laws of Success* (San Rafael, CA: Amber-Allen Publishing and New World Library, 1994).

Dr. Wayne W. Dyer, *The Power of Intention* (Carlsbad, CA: Hay House, 2004).

Marianne Williamson, *The Gift of Change* (San Francisco, CA: HarperCollins, 2004).

Gary Zukav, *The Seat of the Soul* (New York, NY: Simon & Schuster, 1989).

Chapter 1: Creating Your Own Luck
Reprinted from Carl Holmes, *And Then Some . . .*, The Executive Gallery, Inc. plaque.

Chapter 2: Don't Be Blowing in the Wind
Henry C. Fountain, "Even Cardinals Are Prone to Peer

Pressure," *New York Times*, 17 April 2005. Copyright © 2005 by The New York Times Co. Reprinted with permission.

Laurence G. Boldt, *Zen Soul* (New York, NY: Penguin Group, 1997), pp. 6-7.

Brian Tracy, "The Indispensable Quality," *Jim Rohn's Weekly E-zine*, 243 (June 2004).

Khaled Hosseini, *The Kite Runner* (New York, NY: Berkley Publishing Group, 2003), p. 55.

Fred Rogers, *The World According to Mr. Rogers* (New York, NY: Hyperion Books, 2003), p. 42.

Chapter 3: Seeing the Elephant

Alex Stone, "School of Flock," *Discover* (May 2005). Excerpted with permission from the May 1, 2005, issue of *Discover* magazine. Copyright © Discover Magazine.

Chapter 4: The Stories You Tell

Jennie Renton, "The Story Behind the Potter Legend," *Sydney Morning Herald*, 28 October 2001, http://www.accio-quote.org/articles/2001/1001-sydney-renton.htm.

Annette Simmons, *The Story Factor* (New York, NY: Perseus Books, 2001), pp. 5, 39, 108. Reprinted by permission of Basic Books, a member of Perseus Books Group.

Kay Young and Jeffrey L. Savor, "The Neurology of Narrative." (Presentation March 6, 1998). Abstract, http://www.anth.ucsb.edu/projects/esm/YoungSaver.html.

T. Harv Eker, *Secrets of the Millionaire Mind* (New York, NY: HarperCollins Publishers, 2005), p. 113.

Kyle Maynard, *No Excuses* (Washington, DC: Regnery Publishing, 2006).

Pamela Babcock, "Is Your Company Two-Faced?" *HR Magazine*, 49, No. 1, (January 2004), http://www.shrm.org/hrmagazine/articles/0104/0104covstory.asp.

Peg C. Neuhauser, *Corporate Legends & Lore* (New York, NY: McGraw-Hill, 1993), p. 27.

Chapter 5: It's Not About You

Reprinted with permission of Fast Company, from "Was

Built to Last Built to Last," Jennifer Reingold and Ryan Underwood, 2004; permission conveyed through Copyright Clearance Center, Inc.

Chapter 6: It's All About You
"Show Me" from *My Fair Lady*. Words by Alan Jay Lerner, Music by Frederick Loewe, © 1956 (Renewed) Alan Jay Lerner and Frederick Loewe. Publication and Allied Rights Assigned to Chappell & Co. Used by permission of Alfred Publishing Co., Inc.

Mark R. Leary, *The Curse of the Self* (New York, NY: Oxford University Press, 2004), pp. 57-59, 67. By permission of Oxford University Press, Inc.

Lyrics to "Future Games" (Welch) reprinted with permission from Crosstown Songs LLC.

Chapter 7: Bringing Yourself to Work
Peanuts: ©United Feature Syndicate, Inc. Used by Permission.

Sharon Jayson, "The Goal: Wealth and Fame," *USA Today*, 10 January 2007. From *USA Today*, a division of Gannett Co., Inc. Reprinted with permission.

Jesse McKinley, "Broadway Debut for Julia Roberts," *New York Times*, 29 July 2005. Copyright © 2005 by The New York Times Co. Reprinted with permission.

Chapter 8: A Practice of Trust
David Cay Johnson, "IRS Is Losing Its War on Tax Cheats," *New York Times*, 11 May 2002. Copyright © 2002 by The New York Times Co. Reprinted with permission.

Bridgid Schulte, "Cheatin' Writin' and Rithmetic," *Washington Post*, 15 September 2002, p. W16. Reprinted with permission.

Matt Villano, "Served as King of England, Said the Resume," *New York Times*, 19 March 2006. Copyright © 2006 by The New York Times Co. Reprinted with permission.

Nancy Kalish, "How Honest Are You?" *Readers Digest* (January 2004), http://www.rd.com/content/how-honest-are-you/.

Kate Lorenz, "Is Your Boss Spying on You?" *CNN.com*, 24

March 2005. Copyright © 2005 CareerBuilders.com. Reprinted with permission.

Scott Medintz, "The Lies We Tell," *CNNMoney.com*, 11 March 2005. Used with permission.

Milt Freudenheim and Mary Williams Walsh, "The Next Retirement Time Bomb," *New York Times*, 11 December 2005. Copyright © 2005 by The New York Times Co. Reprinted with permission.

"Sign of the Times," *American Demographics* (June 2003).

Natalie Angier, "Why We're So Nice: We're Wired to Cooperate," *New York Times*, 23 July 2002. Copyright © 2002 by The New York Times Co. Reprinted with permission.

Jack R. Gibb, *Trust: A New View of Personal and Organizational Development* (Los Angeles, CA: The Guild of Tutors Press, 1978), p. 10.

Robert C. Solomon and Fernando Flores, *Building Trust in Business, Politics, Relationships and Life* (New York, NY: Oxford University Press, 2001), pp. 7, 55-59, 95-102, 118, 135. By permission of Oxford University Press, Inc.

Jeanne Sahadi, "You May Be Paid More (or Less) Than You Think," *CNNMoney.com*, 29 March 2006. Used with permission.

Watson Wyatt, *WorkUSA® 2002 - Weathering the Storm: A Study of Employee Attitudes and Opinions* (Watson Wyatt Worldwide, 2002), http://www.watsonwyatt.com/research/resrender.asp?id=W-557&page=1.

Robert Galford and Anne Seibold Drapeau, *The Trust Leader* (New York, NY: The Free Press, 2002).

Dennis S. Reina & Michelle L. Reina, *Trust & Betrayal in the Workplace* (San Francisco, CA: Berrett-Koehler Publishers, 1999).

Chapter 9: Shades of Grey

Doris Kearns Goodwin, *Team of Rivals* (New York, NY: Simon & Schuster, 2005), pp. 170-172.

Associated Press, "Sex, Shopping and Gambling All in a Day's Work. Used with permission of The Associated Press Copyright © 2007.

Dr. Fred Luskin, *Forgive for Good* (San Francisco, CA:

HarperCollins, 2002), pp. 46-57. Very brief quotations as submitted from *Forgive for Good: A Proven Prescription for Health and Happiness* by Dr. Fred Luskin. Copyright © 2002 by Frederick Luskin. Reprinted by permission of Harper Collins Publishers.

Chapter 10: Waking Up
Disney Enterprises, Disney's *Add a Little Magic, Words of Inspiration* (New York, NY: Disney Press, 1999). Excerpts from the script of Walt Disney's copyrighted feature film PINOCCHIO are used by permission from Disney Enterprises, Inc.

ONLY FOR YOU . . .
HITTING YOUR STRIDE
SPECIAL GIFTS

My hope is that this book speeds your journey to finding and *hitting your stride*, enhances your work life, and encourages you to live your life's dreams.

I'd like to continue helping you reach your life's potential. So I created three gifts to thank you for investing in *Hitting Your Stride.*

To help you get the full value from this book, there's a collection of *free* extra resources waiting for you at www.hittingyourstridenow.com:

HITTING YOUR STRIDE TOOLBOX— THREE FREE GIFTS

1. *How to Get the Life You Want*—Audio Download— "Knowledge Tool"
   - ★ Nan's powerful technique for actualizing your dreams
   - ★ How to create the future you want without working harder
   - ★ The big mistakes that hold most people back
   - ★ Increase your happiness and well-being

2. *Finding Your Stride*—Online Interactive—"Self-Assessment Tool"
   - ★ Calculate your SQ—stride quotient
   - ★ What now? Stride Tips
   - ★ Maximize your work flexibility and choices
   - ★ Use your uniqueness at work and make a difference

3. *Your Personal Dream-Maker*—PDF Download—"Reflective Planning Tool"
   ★ Move in the direction of your dreams at a pace right for you
   ★ Stepped approach to building the future you want
   ★ Offer the best of who you are and be rewarded with interesting work
   ★ Do what most people never do by creating your own life luck

Wishing you dreams come true,

Nan S. Russell
info@nanrussell.com
www.nanrussell.com

INDEX

About the Author
Nan S. Russell

With a bachelors from Stanford and a masters from the University of Michigan, Nan was fired from her first professional job. Taking a minimum wage job to pay the rent, sixteen promotions and twenty years in management later, she ended her corporate career as a vice president with multibillion dollar QVC, to pursue a life dream to live and write from the mountains of Montana. Now a columnist, author, and speaker, Nan is living her dream by helping others to live theirs. More about Nan and her work can be found at www.nanrussell.com.